THESE SPINDRIFT PAGES

THESE SPINDRIFT PAGES

THEODORE DALRYMPLE

MIRABEAU PRESS

Published by Mirabeau Press

PO Box 4281

West Palm Beach, FL 33401

ISBN: 978-1-7357055-5-2

First Edition

MIRABEAU

Not for ambition or bread
Or the strut and trade of charms
On the ivory stages
But for the common wages
Of their most secret heart.
Not for the proud man apart
From the raging moon I write
On these spindrift pages…

In My Craft or Sullen Art, Dylan Thomas

Some years ago, my wife gave me a beautiful and expensive notebook of thick paper and gilt-edged pages. It was too good for mundane use, and for long it stood empty as a reproach to my lack of industry or inspiration. Finally, I decided to employ it to record thoughts about what I read for, having led a fairly active life, I have for some years lived mainly through books, which I read in dialectical relationship, as it were, with my accumulated experience.

I have no grand theory to propound. I have no key either to the meaning of life or to the way in which it should be lived. Insofar as I have a point to make, it is that any moderately-sized library has within it enough to provide more than sufficient interest for a hundred lifetimes. Pascal said that much of the trouble of mankind came from the inability of people to be at peace alone in a room. Much of its boredom (an underestimated mischief-maker) derives from its inability to find satisfaction in a shelf of books.

The length of this work was determined precisely by the size of the notebook. I started on the first line and determined to end on the last. I kept to my plan, except that the last line was written in the lower margin of the last page.

For reasons not to my purpose here, I was reading *Wittgenstein: A Religious Perspective?* by the American philosopher, Norman Malcolm, when I had the kind of moment described by Proust, though in this case not caused by the odour of a madeleine but by a small mark in pencil opposite the half-title page of the book.

I had bought the book at least a quarter of a century earlier

(I buy books much faster than I read them but never without the intention of one day doing so). I recognised the small mark at once: it was the price scribbled in pencil by S...... W........, a dealer in second-hand books from whom I first bought such books between forty and fifty years ago as I write this. I should recognise his writing anywhere, especially on the inside of a book.

Unlike some dealers, he had a light touch with his pencil so that its mark could be erased without leaving a trace on the page. He had a light touch in other respects too. Many times, I witnessed him refusing to buy a collection of rubbishy airport novels from hopeful sellers without giving the faintest hint of the disdain he actually felt and which he expressed after the would-be vendors' departure. Could such people not see that he did not sell such cheap and trashy books? But he was unfailingly, almost ceremoniously, polite to their faces in order not to offend.

In the days before the internet (O, how long ago!), he would take a pile of books and attach a price to them at a glance. In many years of conversation with him I do not recall ever having mentioned a book of which he had not heard or of which he knew absolutely nothing. Presumably his knowledge was often superficial, for I never saw him engrossed for long in a book. He must have acquired the art of absorbing much from a paragraph as he priced a book. He could remember exactly when the rarer volumes had passed through his hands.

His literary judgments were sound and above all interesting. It was he who pointed out to me that the cheap novels of the 1920s and 30s were often well-written, much better than their counterparts today. When I looked into it, I found that he was right. What did this mean? That the reading public of nearly a century ago was better-educated and more demanding than it is today? Or was it that those who took to the pen in those days were fewer than today, and better educated? Perhaps the audience was smaller and more select. Or again, perhaps our vastly increased technical sophistication has not necessarily led to an increased mental sophistication; and literacy is not proportional to the years spent in education.

One day, I happened to discuss with him the question of whether doctors were especially apt to become good writers. In such discussions, people are inclined to indulge in list competition, and we were no exception, starting with the most obvious — Chekhov, Somerset Maugham — and ending with the lesser-known medical writers, poets such as Samuel Garth and Mark Akenside. Mr W…….. said that there seemed to be a connection between medicine as a profession and the urge to write, whereupon I was seized by the fashionable requirement that all such generalisations should be supported by statistical evidence.

'Doctors,' I said, 'are educated. 'How many writers do you expect to find among the educated?'

In other words, unless you could show that more doctors than expected for their social class and level of education had been writers, claims of a special relationship between medicine as a profession and writing would be hollow. Mr W…….. thought for a moment.

'How many writers do you know who were dentists?' he asked.

A brilliant, incisive reply.

Mostly it was cold in his shop, even when it was hot outside, with that kind of penetrating cold that is impossible to drive out and that seems more a positive quality than a mere absence of warmth. He would sit in the centre of the shop by a feeble paraffin fire in a thick pullover that ended in mittens. He was joined by his wife, whom he married relatively late in life, who was also a bookseller who wore mittens. At least the cold kept the insects down.

One day, however, it was so hot outside that some warmth managed to penetrate the shop and Mr W........ was in his shirt-sleeves. I still remember the shock of the discovery that he had a blue tattoo on one of his forearms. In those days, one did not know people who had tattoos; the fashion for them was still years off and was confined to sailors, criminals and (so it was alleged) to degenerate aristocrats. How and why did Mr W........ come by his tattoo? I had spoken to him often, entered his shop dozens of times, yet how little did I know him! Each of us has a hinterland unknown to others. Thank goodness! A transparent life would be intolerable, as well as shallow.

Should I erase the price in the book written in pencil? I dislike such disfigurements — marginal annotations are another thing. But to erase it would be to erase a little part of my own past, or at least a stimulus to my memory of my own past. The mark, of course, will mean nothing to whoever comes to own the book after my demise, assuming that the book itself will not simply be thrown away. Meanings borne by such slight or trivial indications are not transferable from one person to another. They form, as Wittgenstein would not have said, a private language.

The concluding paragraph of the editor's introduction to *The Trial of Patrick Herbert Mahon* is as follows:

> There never was a more cold-blooded murderer, except perhaps George Joseph Smith, than this unspeakable villain. Even at the end, when he confessed his guilt to the prison officials [just before he was hanged], he begged that they would not make public his confession for fear of the "bad impression it might make."

The editor of the book was none other than Edgar Wallace, one of the pulp writers to whom Mr W…….. referred, and among the most successful financially if not stylistically. For twenty-five years he wrote four books a year and would have made an immense fortune had he not been so spendthrift. He was the subject of one of the best literary biographies that I have ever read, by Margaret Lane, a masterpiece of tone and tact, judicious as to length, and sympathetic without being hagiographic.

Edgar Wallace never aspired to literary praise: he wanted to make money and made it, even if his bank accounts were leaking buckets. The surprising thing is that he was any kind of writer at all, for he left school at the age of twelve, as his economic circumstances dictated, to earn his own living. Presumably, elementary education in the slums was better in his day than in ours, for it is difficult to imagine any twelve-year-old school- leaver (even if such existed) becoming a writer, even one of Edgar Wallace's standard. And after all, a number of his books are still in print after a hundred years.

As for Patrick Herbert Mahon, he was indeed a cold-blooded murderer. He killed his paramour, Emily Kaye, during what he called 'a love experiment' in a bungalow that he had rented for the purpose just outside Eastbourne. He bludgeoned her to death, probably because a) she was pregnant by him and b) she was threatening to expose him unless he ran away with her to South Africa, which he had no desire or intention to do. According to Edgar Wallace, whose interest in crime was assiduous and whose knowledge of it was extensive, Mahon was then faced with the problem which has faced many a murderer, namely the disposal of the body. He was in no great hurry, however, for with Miss Kaye's body still in the bungalow, he invited another paramour down to the seaside. He disposed of at least some of the body — the head was never found — from the windows of the train back to London.

Is it not strange that such a man should be worried about the impression his confession might make? He was a psychopath who craved respectability. I was about to say that one doesn't meet murderers these days half as interesting, but I recall one who said to me, 'I had to kill her, doctor, or I don't know what I would have done.'

I have a fair number of books about the death penalty but, insofar as I know the contents of my own library, only two in its favour, the rest passionately against. In a way this is odd, because at the time of its abolition, the great majority of the population was in favour of its retention, at least in Britain and France. But it is always the reformers, or would-be reformers, who write the books; those in favour of the *status quo* are always less prolific. The preponderance, then, is not so surprising.

The first of the two pro-death penalty books was given to me (with a dedication) by a lawyer in New Zealand. The second — *Oui à la peine de mort*, Yes to the Death Penalty — was by a Dominican priest, Richard-Louis Bruckberger, and was published in 1985, four years after the abolition in France. Ever since the abolition, the French political class has behaved as if the abolition took place in 1981 B.C. rather than in A.D. 1981, so brutal and primitive does it accuse countries of being that retain the death penalty (though rarely mentioning Japan among them).

Bruckberger's arguments are very old-fashioned. He does not enter into statistics, saying that they can prove anything, or at least be used to prove anything (not the same thing, of course). He is hardly concerned with practical questions such as whether the death penalty is effective as a deterrent. The nearest he comes to such a view is to mention a few cases of murder which, had the death penalty been applied after the murderer's first offence, would have been avoided.

His arguments are philosophical and even theological. He points out that the Gospels nowhere enjoin forgiveness of those who wrong others: indeed, forgiveness is possible only by the person wronged. Therefore, the state has no standing to exercise forgiveness, only mercy. The latter, however, must be exercised with prudence and judgment. Mercy towards, say, Himmler (had he not killed himself), would have been unthinking and unfeeling.

I had assumed that Bruckberger was ultramontane, perhaps a member of *Opus Dei*, but I was mistaken. He had been a member of the Resistance and close to de Gaulle. After the war, he was so appalled by the *épuration*, the means by which revenge was often taken on collaborators, alleged collaborators and private enemies, that he was at first firmly opposed to the death penalty. But as times became more normal, at least in metropolitan France, he changed his mind.

The need for vengeance, he realised, was part of human nature and a legitimate part of it. Without vengeance there could be no justice. Moreover, people have an inalienable *right* to be punished: for without punishment there can be no desert, and without desert there can be no justice or freedom (his argument approaches, much less lucidly, that of another Christian writer, C.S. Lewis, in his essay *The Humanitarian Theory of Punishment*). We have, however, handed over to the state the business of talking vengeance on wrongdoers, which Bruckberger, surely with reason, considers an essential advance in civilisation.

Is Bruckberger being inconsistent? After all, if one can outsource vengeance to the state, why not forgiveness? If it is argued that a crime is also a crime against society or the state, and that this gives it every right to exercise vengeance, and not merely as a sub-contractor, as it were, then surely it has the right to exercise forgiveness also. But perhaps vengeance and forgiveness are not mirror images, or goose and gander.

Rather surprisingly, Bruckberger does not consider the undoubted phenomenon of wrongful execution, no matter how scrupulous the jurisdiction. The usual argument is that such wrongful executions are very few and outnumbered by the number of second murders committed by persons who should have been executed the first time round. This argument depends on the correctness, as a moral theory, of some kind of utilitarianism — though the argument, in my view, serves more as a refutation of utilitarianism.

There is one passage in the book that is of particular salience today (it seems to me):

> It is not only territories that can be violated and occupied by the enemy. There is also the language, 'the holy language', that can perhaps be profaned and besmirched, so to speak, by a foreign occupation, an occupation that is the enemy, the murderer of sense. The sign by which I recognise a real writer is that he does not accept the profanation of the sanctuary of language: his unceasing combat is to liberate words from the yoke that weighs on them.

No doubt it is absurd for a man of my age to harbour any ambitions at all, but still I should like to catalogue my books before I die. This is a foolish ambition, even by ambition's standards, for my executors will almost certainly rid themselves of my library as soon as they are able, in the most convenient and expeditious way possible, no doubt involving much destruction.

Nevertheless, Mr David Tudor having kindly created a database for me, I have started to catalogue my books. It takes between two and three hours to catalogue forty books, and if I take this time every day for the next two or three years, I shall have succeeded, if I do not die first. I know myself too well, however, not to entertain the possibility of abandonment well before accomplishment.

As I catalogue my books, I find those that I have never read, those that I have read and remember, those that I have read and don't remember, and those that I cannot even remember whether or not I have read them (by definition, I don't remember their contents, though I may know something about them). In the latter category was a book by Thierry Desjardins, former editor-in-chief of the French newspaper, *Le Figaro*, titled *Assez! de mensonges, d'hypocrisie de promesses, de parlotes, de trahisons, de lâcheté* (Enough! of Lies, Hypocrisy, Promises, Verbiage, Betrayal, Cowardice). Amen to that, I thought: but who actually wants *more* lies, *more* hypocrisy, etc.?

Enough! begins:

> Never has the situation of our country been as catastrophic as it is today. We have been saying so for decades, but it has been true, unfortunately, for years, since everything worsens from month to month.

Though I am no optimist, this rather gloomy assessment doesn't strike me as strictly accurate, but accuracy does not immediately attract many readers (or purchasers, overlapping populations but not identical). 'Our country has many problems, like all countries, and as it always has' is not the kind of beginning that would grip many people. Readers want catastrophe, nothing less. All judgment is comparative, said Doctor Johnson, which makes the choice of comparator so important. When one says, 'Never has been', one should really add 'since'. What about the Wars of Religion in France, in which millions lost their lives? The Franco-Prussian War and its aftermath? The Occupation? The Terror? Or does the author mean 'Never in the last thirty years'? Certainly, the author, in the following paragraphs, makes France sound like a living hell, which clearly it is not. Anyone who thinks that France is a living hell has never been to Merthyr Tydfil, and anyone who thinks Merthyr Tydfil is a living hell has never been to….

Enough! *Enough!* was published in 2006. What is strange reading it now — it is instructive to read the ephemera of a few years ago — is that what it says is exactly what like-minded people say fifteen years later. The same complaints, in the same language, with the same evidence in support:

> Those French who stay [having failed to depart for greener, less highly-taxed pastures elsewhere] form two Frances that despise each other, that hate each other. There are those, totally discouraged, crushed by taxes, fearing unemployment or bankruptcy, seeing their standard of living declining year after year, who lament, despair and dream only of one thing: that everything should explode so as to finish at last this absurd, suffocating, sterile system…
>
> And then it is true, there are those who profit from it, the beneficiaries of the system, the salaried public sector workers, civil servants, or employees of public enterprises, who have guaranteed employment and all the advantages… and who block all idea of reform…

And this could have been written, word for word, fifteen years later — or before, for that matter.

I am put in mind of a conversation I had with my barber in Paris. He is, if not my hero exactly, at least heroic. He is of Moroccan origin, having emigrated to France as a young man. His French, as far as I am able to judge, is perfect, without accent; he is clearly intelligent and one suspects that, in another life and in other circumstances, he might have done 'better' that to run a single-handed barber's shop in the 20th Arrondissement of Paris. This is not certain, however, for he is as modest, or perhaps timid, as he is intelligent. He is one of those many people, hardworking and uncomplaining, upon whose labour the possibility of an agreeable and civilised life depends.

'Since I arrived in this country,' he said as he cut my hair, or what is left of it, and we discussed the forthcoming election, 'I have heard the same debates about the same subjects using the same arguments.'

I laughed.

'It is the same everywhere,' I said.

'France,' he continued, 'is like a man who has complained of toothache for twenty-five years but has never found the time to go to the dentist.'

A brilliant formulation.

As it happens, on the day on which I catalogued the book by Desjardins, the man who cuts the trees around our house in the Ardèche came to look at what needed to be done this year in the way of tree-cutting. A man in his mid-forties, he lamented the fact that it was uneconomic for him to take on an employee, though he had more work than he could cope with. The employee might prove to be no good, but French labour law would make it expensive and time-consuming to dismiss him. Besides, he said, young people nowadays didn't want to work.

'We have raised a generation of good-for-nothings,' he said.

'They probably said that two thousand years ago,' I said.

'Yes,' he replied. 'Two thousand years of good-for-nothings!'

Pottering in my library, I came across another book with the writing of S...... W........ in it (it doesn't matter which, but it was *Cholera, 1832* by R.J. Morris). And this brought to mind another conversation that I had with him that opened my eyes to another aspect of the wickedness of the world.

I entered his shop one day and he was sitting at his desk as usual, but he was in an unaccustomed state of agitation. He was reading a little booklet.

'Look at this!' he said.

'What is it?' I asked.

'The annual accounts of Oxfam.'

He pushed the booklet over to me. I looked at the table of figures. I was not an habitual decipherer of accounts.

'Well?' I asked.

'Well what?'

I had seen but not observed, so he explained to me. Oxfam, the charity, ran many shops of donated goods, including books, so many in fact that it was affecting the second-hand book trade adversely. But despite the fact that its goods were free to it, that most of the staff of the shops were unpaid volunteers, and that the shops had low concessionary rates of local taxation, their rate of gross profit was only 17 per cent. How was this possible, when he, who had to pay for his goods, pay staff (admittedly only part-time), and pay high local taxes, made — and had to make, in order for his business to be viable at all — a rate of gross profit of 35 per cent? Where did all the rest of the money taken in Oxfam's shops go?

Where indeed? I began habitually to look into the trading accounts of other charities and found many to be even worse. In one year that I looked, the gross profit of the shops run by the British Red Cross was a mere 8 per cent: that is to say, only 8 per cent of their turnover was actually passed to the British Red Cross itself, and of that 8 per cent, probably a half was expended on administration and staff. I went into one of these shops and bought a book for £1. I asked the old ladies at the till who had volunteered their services how much of my pound went to the British Red Cross. They were shocked by my question, which presumably they thought was an implicit accusation of wrongdoing by themselves.

'All of it of course,' one of them said.

I did not disillusion them: it would have been cruel to do so. They thought, or imagined, that by volunteering, they were bringing some relief to those poor who had suffered a catastrophe, while at the same time getting out of the house and enjoying some social life. Still, I could not but be a little outraged by this exploitation of the goodwill of these old ladies, probably widows.

There were other deformations of charity in the traditional sense that I discovered. The word *charity* was used in such a way as to retain its original connotation but that was empty of its original content (a characteristic modern form of dishonesty). For example, a charity called the Child Poverty Action Group obtained almost all of its income from governmental sources, which it used to lobby the government to spend more money on reducing child poverty. Irrespective of whether this proposed extra expenditure was wise or good, this amounted to the government lobbying itself to increase its expenditure: a very far cry from charity as most people conceive it.

When I drew public attention to this, the charity replied that it fulfilled the legal criteria for a charity to be considered as such. This amounted, so it seemed to me, to the argument often heard in defence of some disagreeable or antisocial behaviour, that 'There is no law against it'. In other words, the law, and the law alone, determines what it is right and proper to do. We have outsourced moral judgment.

In a letter dated 9 January, 1889, to his friend, publisher and advisor, A.S. Suvorin, Anton Chekhov went straight to the heart of Man's mystery, without plucking it out: in my opinion, no one will ever be able to do that.

> Write a story of how a young man, the son of a serf, who has served in a shop, sung in a choir, been at a high school and a university, who has been brought up to respect everyone of higher rank and position, to kiss priests' hands, to reverence other people's ideas, to be thankful for every morsel of bread, who has been many times whipped, who has trudged from one pupil to another without galoshes, who has been used to fighting,

and tormenting animals, who has liked dining with rich relations, and been hypocritical before God and man from mere consciousness of his own insignificance – write how this young man squeezes the slave out of himself drop by drop, and how waking one beautiful morning he feels that he has no longer a slave's blood in his veins but a real man's...

How do we become what we are, and what part, exactly, do we play in becoming what we are? Chekhov implies that he *chose* to free himself from his circumstances and that if he so willed it, those circumstances would not determine any longer his character or actions. This being the case, he could no longer make excuses for himself; henceforth he was, as W.E. Henley put it in a poem published less than a year before Chekhov's letter, 'The master of his fate, the captain of his soul.'

But surely it takes character to build one's character? How does one develop the necessary character to develop one's character? Are we not faced by an infinite regress of characters that build character to build character? If we choose not to squeeze the slave from ourselves drop by drop, or do not even realise that it is a choice not to do so, is our enslavement to our circumstances real or false, a mere rationalisation? I hear objectors in my mind's ear saying, 'It was all very well for Chekhov to talk, he was a genius, but most people have no special talent or ability, and they are not even very intelligent.'

We do not live in times very propitious to a belief in the self-creating nature of human character. Once we have said heredity and environment, we have said everything that can be said. What else can go to the explanation of human conduct and character? And yet how thin and unsatisfactory an explanation sounds once we have applied it to an individual! All such explanations, however plausible, are *ex post facto*: they are useless for predictive purposes. What in Anton Pavlovich's genes or environment would have allowed us to predict the authorship of *The Cherry Orchard*?

Some are more interested in the future than the past, and some are more interested in the past than the future. I am of the latter type or school, not because of some general belief that the past was better, but because it suits me temperamentally. Most people's opinions depend at least as much on their temperament as upon abstract principle, and such principles as they adopt are often by elective affinity.

The future is radically unknown, the past only relatively so. In fact, it is sometimes better known than the present, whose dust needs to settle before it can be properly appreciated. And the study of the past is consolatory: it reminds us that our present travails may not be unprecedented or even the worst ever experienced, and that we are not as alone in them as we had liked to suppose.

As an expert witness in a number of murder trials, I was naturally interested in the testimony of my predecessors in the genre, my colleagues by antecedence as it were. An American historian, Joel Peter Eigen, has written several books about the development of psychiatric testimony in English courts in the nineteenth century. I opened one of them recently, *Unconscious Crime: Mental Absence and Criminal Responsibility*, and was intrigued by a chapter heading, *An Unconscious Poisoning*.

Can one really poison somebody in a fit of absence of mind? One is not talking here of ignorance: of someone who adds an ingredient without knowing that its effect is deadly, as a fond dog-owner might give his dog dark chocolate from unawareness of its potential effect. One is talking rather of someone who adds a known poison to food or drink, a seemingly intentional and planned act, supposedly in a state of trance or automatism. And if it is done, is the person the less culpable because of it? How does one estimate the reality of the exculpatory altered state of consciousness, which after all anybody can claim after having committed the heinous deed? Many a prisoner on remand for some heinous crime told me that he couldn't have been guilty of it because he couldn't remember having done it. If memory is crucial to personal identity, as many philosophers have argued, or if personal identity is an illusion, as some others have also argued, then every such crime must have been committed by someone other than the accused, who is not guilty because of the passage of time since it was committed.

'If you can't remember,' I would say to the prisoner on remand, 'you're not in a very strong position to deny the evidence against you, are you?'

Sometimes their memories would then undergo a miraculous improvement. And drunkenness of such a degree as to result in memory impairment traditionally is not a legal excuse however genuine the impairment might be.

The case of unconscious poisoning brought forward for examination by Professor Eigen was really nothing of the kind. It was that of William Newton Allnut, a twelve-year-old boy who, in 1847, put arsenic in the sugar that he knew that his grandfather would sprinkle on his baked apple. This was his second go at poisoning him; according to the prosecution, he coveted his grandfather's gold watch, gold-framed eyeglasses, and his gold sovereigns, which presumably he thought that he would inherit, or at least be able to take possession of. Covetousness, it seems, develops, or can develop, early in life.

Evidence was brought forth at his trial that little William had always been a bad boy, completely without scruple and utterly amoral. Even his mother said so. Indeed, she had opposed bail for her son, considering him too dangerous to be left at liberty. While imprisoned, he wrote a letter to his mother (at least as well written than most 12-year-olds would manage today, I suspect):

> I confess to what I am accused of. How I got the poison was this: on the 20th October Grandfather went to his desk for the key to the wine cellar to get some wine up, and while he was gone I took the poison out and emptied some of it into another piece of paper, and put the other back; and then after dinner I put it in the sugar basin; and why I did it was I had made Grandfather angry with something I had done and he Knocked me down in the passage… If I am transported [to Van Diemen's Land, now Tasmania] I know it will be the death of me, therefore I hope they will pardon me. With kindest love to you and all at home, believe me, your affectionate son, W.N.A.

If it were not for his tender age, we should have no hesitation in calling him a psychopath, that is to say someone constitutionally without conscience: someone who might appreciate cognitively the difference between right and wrong, as we appreciate the difference between the Coleoptera and the Hymenoptera, between the beetles and the ants, bees and wasps, but who is incapable of seeing why the difference should guide his behaviour. Some of the doctors at the time of William's trial said that his indifference to right and wrong was a quasi-neurological condition, but the jury took no notice and convicted him anyway, though recommending mercy on the grounds of his youth. His death sentence was indeed commuted on these grounds, and he was imprisoned for life, or sentenced to such. Unfortunately, Professor Eigen does not tell us of his subsequent career, if it may be so-called.

There do seem to be people who are constitutionally bad: that is to say who, from an early age, are completely without moral restraint. They are cruel to animals, lie and steal, often without obvious benefit to themselves, are undeterred by past or future punishment, and are unmoved by appeals to their finer feelings, of which they have none. If they change for the better, it is only with the passage of time, and not because of any change of heart or of any medical treatment.

Are they fully responsible for their actions? They know what they are doing, they know that it is wrong in the sense that others will reprehend it, but they are by nature prevented from caring. The problem, or puzzle, has not been solved two centuries after doctors first drew attention to it.

I was once involved in a trial of a woman who had poisoned to death her two-year-old child. She had emptied the contents of her antidepressant capsules and dissolved them in a cough syrup that she then spoon-fed to her sleepy child who died as a result. She was tried for murder.

There was neither question nor denial of her having committed the acts of which she was accused: the only question at issue was whether she was fully responsible for them. She was an alcoholic who had conceived rather later in life by another alcoholic of her drunken acquaintance. Rather surprisingly, he changed his ways after the child's birth and thenceforth eschewed drink, but she did not. As a result of this disparity, he applied for sole custody of the child on the grounds that the mother was unfit to look after it. The court was about to hear his application, which she feared might be granted, and it was then that she killed the child. I surmised that she told herself that if she could not keep the child, no one would: the kind of jealous avowal that has preceded many the murder of a supposedly unfaithful lover. 'If I can't have her, no one else will,' goes the refrain.

I argued that she had no medical excuse or mitigation for what she had done, albeit — or especially because — she had been drinking. It was argued to the contrary — successfully — that she suffered from a personality disorder that limited her responsibility. She had long been an inadequate person in many respects, and her chronic inadequacy rendered her less culpable than she would otherwise have been. This view prevailed: she was found guilty of a lesser charge and sentenced to what in effect was eighteen months' imprisonment.

The logic of all this seemed to me peculiar, and not only because of the circular nature of the diagnosis and the conduct: we know she had, or was, a personality disorder because of the way she behaved, and she behaved the way she did because she had, or was, a personality disorder. But if it was really believed that she killed because of her personality disorder, which as a matter of experience and empirical fact was permanent and incurable, then she would have remained a very dangerous person, whom nothing would prevent from striking again should the circumstance be right, and who therefore (from the public safety point of view) required long incarceration. In fact, neither I nor anyone else thought that she was likely to kill again, because the circumstances in which she killed were unlikely ever to arise again. But her action in killing was a planned and thought-out one, premeditated if premeditation means anything. Eighteen months' imprisonment for such an act (formally, the sentence was three years, but fifty per cent remission is now automatic in England, almost a fundamental human right) seemed at least as inadequate as the culprit's personality. If eighteen months' imprisonment is the punishment for deliberately poisoning a child to death, what can the punishment be for lesser, but still very serious, crimes?

If it is argued that her sentence should have been short because a) she regretted her act, which she made somewhat histrionically clear throughout her trial by wailing the name of her dead child, such that her name is engraved forever on my memory, and b) she was unlikely ever to do anything similar again, consider the following scenario. Heinrich Himmler did not commit suicide but was captured, survived and faced trial. He now says that he truly regrets what he did and caused to be done and realises that it is totally wrong to kill millions of people in gas chambers, or by working them to death in camps. He promises never to do it again, besides which the new circumstances in which Germany finds itself make it impossible for him to do so. Would we say, 'Well, no justification for punishing him, then?' I think not.

As I write this, the journalist and polemicist Éric Zemmour is still a candidate for the Presidency of France. As a long-term observer of the political scene, he must know that his chances of success are approximately nil (thank goodness), but he probably intends by his candidature to spread his ideas like a gaseous effusion into the political atmosphere. Here he is more likely to be successful.

I saw him once give a talk in Budapest. The former President, Nicolas Sarkozy, spoke at the same conference. The latter was passionate, jumping up and down and flinging his arms about like a marionette under only the partial control of its puppeteer. What he said was immediately forgettable; indeed, one forgot it even before he had finished saying it. I likened him to a dried pea being shaken in a tin box.

Zemmour, by contrast, was obviously a more serious, if sinister, figure, a small, swarthy man who seemed eaten up by something and definitely gave off the whiff of sulphur. There was something almost Mephistophelian about him. I have no indisputable grounds for saying this, but I felt that I should not like to be in his power.

He spoke as passionately as Sarkozy but, unlike Sarkozy, what he said had content, agree or disagree with it as you might. Zemmour is a fluent, practised and powerful speaker, whose logic is often impeccable: it is just that his premises are often extreme assertions untroubled by nuance or complexity. His obsessions are, or have become, well-known: the decline of the prestige of France, thanks to the antipatriotic treachery of its elites, to its de-industrialisation, and above all to the deliberate dilution of French traditions and culture brought about by mass immigration, above all Muslim immigration from North Africa (Zemmour's parents were Jewish Berber immigrants from Morocco, fleeing from fear of the post-independence Moroccan state).

No doubt Zemmour's all but unqualified detestation not only of Islam but of Moslem immigrants is what also accounts for the detestation that he himself arouses. No doubt in addition the refusal of the politico-bureaucratic elite in France even to recognise any problem at all caused by large-scale immigration from Moslem countries made inevitable the ascent of a demagogue. As Stanley Spencer once wrote, 'The suppression of every error is commonly followed by a temporary ascendency of the contrary error.'

Zemmour's evident visceral hatred of Moslems causes me distress whenever I see or hear it and whenever I think of the individual immigrants whom I encounter. It is not that I have any sympathy whatever for political Islam, quite the reverse; the religion itself does not particularly interest me, though its art has often been magnificent and Moslem societies are not without their charms, even if for the most part their purely political traditions have been unattractive from a modern point of view (but life is not all politics). But a dislike of political Islam is not the same as a blanket condemnation of Moslems, and I cannot help but wonder what it must be like to be an ordinary Moslem immigrant or descendent of such, trying merely to lead a quiet, decent, hardworking life, making one's way as best one can in a perfectly law-abiding way, and yet be the object of the constant denigration and hatred of someone like Zemmour, who has a very considerable following: in short, to be despised, hated and feared *ex officio*.

How does my Parisian barber feel about it? I have not dared to ask, but perhaps next time I will.

My expectation, or suspicion, is that Zemmour will prove to be a comet, or even merely a falling meteorite, in the night sky of French politics, a kind of General Boulanger of the twenty-first century, of no lasting historical significance but fascinating while he moves inexorably towards political annihilation. (My predictions are not often accurate.)

Because of this fascination, I bought four short sequential volumes about him by the prolific journalist, Hubert Prolongeau, with the overall title *Mon Année en Zemmourie* (My Year in Zemmouria, or perhaps Zemmouriland). They are subtitled respectively *L'enfance d'un chef* (The Childhood of a Chief), *Éric le cathodique* (Éric the Televisual), *Femmes: mode d'emploi* (Women: Operating Instructions), and *Une haine française* (A French Hatred). While the author acknowledges Zemmour's gifts, if not his virtues, such as intelligence, capacity for work, ability to charm, he clearly dislikes him intensely.

The four little volumes are a chronicle of the author's attempts to trace Zemmour's past and to delineate his character. It was a brilliant marketing ploy of the publisher, Flammarion, to divide the work into four short volumes rather than publish it in one substantial volume. In these times of reduced attention span, to finish reading even a slender volume is taken by the reader as a worthwhile, even remarkable, achievement; by dividing the book into four, the publisher has given the reader four occasions for self-congratulation.

M. Prolongeau's method is that of the investigative journalist: he seeks the testimony of all who have crossed Zemmour's path in any capacity. What he finds is that very few people who have known Zemmour are willing to talk about him, which implies that Zemmour has a kind of terrorising influence that intimidates people into silence about him. Of course, another interpretation might be that people are loyal towards him and know that M. Prolongeau is intent upon a hatchet job.

Certainly, Zemmour is well-connected, despite claiming to be an outsider. His last book, *La France n'a pas dit son dernier mot* (France Has Not Said Its last Word), is largely a catalogue of his lunchtime conversations with eminent persons. When he was insulted in the street by someone who then posted the film of it on Facebook, the President of the Republic, Emmanuel Macron, telephoned him to commiserate. Macron and Zemmour have each other's private telephone numbers, and according to Zemmour, at least, he subsequently had a forty-five minute conversation with the President about the problem of immigration. This is not a story that many true outsiders could recount.[1]

---

[1] In fairness to Zemmour, he was until recently an outsider to the political world in the strictest sense, having been a mere TV and print journalist. It is also interesting that his latest book suggests a new mode of publishing (or a return to one that was current to an

Journalists are, of course, among the least trusted of all people. In the final volume of his year in Zemmouria, the author wrote:

> In a year of hunting the Zemmour, I had a good little bag. If the fledglings flew from the nest of the Le Pens, the large male let himself be taken. Sliding through the bushes... I was able nevertheless to snare two or three baby rabbits. True, the Pardo [Zemmour's lawyer] kept out of reach of my bullets, teasing me from the tree, allowing me to approach before taking off in great silence. True, the big game, the Naulleau [Zemmour's long-term colleague on television], the loner, the Menard [a far-right politician], whose direction it was impossible to predict, the Ruquier [another television presenter], trying to slip by unseen, escaped me.

I am not sure that I would have wanted to speak to, or trusted, the man who wrote the above, with its implication that anyone who did *not* want to speak to him must have a discreditable reason for his reticence.

The first sentence of Maurizio Serra's excellent study of

---

extent in the nineteenth century). Zemmour's books sell in such quantities that he no longer needs a publisher, only a distributor, thus making far more money for himself. The name of his self-publishing enterprise is *Rubempré*, a reference to the main character in Balzac's novel, *Illusions perdues*. No one doubts that Zemmour is a sincere and knowledgeable lover of French literature.

Mussolini, *Le mystère Mussolini*, struck me immediately as rather odd: 'Benito Mussolini always lied, from the beginning to the end of his life, sometimes without even realising it.'

But can that be right? Surely to lie is by definition to make a statement known by the utterer of it to be false, usually (though not always) with the intention to deceive? How can one be said to be lying if one does not know the falsity of what one is saying? Naturally, the question of whether lying is ever justified is another one entirely, to which the summary answer is, *pace* Kant, 'Yes'. All life establishes it beyond reasonable doubt.

While it seems clear that no man can lie without knowing that he is doing so, yet this also seems a little simplistic as to the possibilities offered by human psychology. It implies that a man is either telling the truth or not, with nothing in between. What of self-deception? We all know what it is and recognise it, at least in others, and yet it is philosophically puzzling, for the deceiver is also the deceived. If to be self-deceived is to believe something that one knows to be false,[2] does this not imply that we have (at least) two minds rather than one? But if so, how are they related or reunited as one? I know that when I am angry, I carry on my angry manner after my true anger has dissipated, and yet I should deny it (angrily) if I were accused of such dishonesty or exaggeration.

There are things that one would like to be true, but knows, or merely suspects, not to be so, and yet one is prepared to defend them with vehemence. One rarely abandons a belief

[2]   When my love swears that she is made of truth
        I do believe her though I know she lies…
                              Shakespeare, Sonnet 138

on the first demonstration of its falsity, especially if one has been emotionally attached to it. And indeed there is a certain rationality to this, for the demonstration of its falsity may itself be false. The precise moment at which it is rational to give up a belief is to an extent dependent on the circumstances. To be too ready to relinquish one's beliefs is to be blown about like a feather in the wind; too stubborn a retention of it is to be dishonest or ossified. Bertrand Russell said that the rational man was he whose beliefs were held with a strength proportional to the evidence in their favour: in which case I would venture to suggest that no rational man has ever lived.

But to return to the question of lying: is everything that we assert either true (in the sense of being an expression of what we believe to be true) or a lie? We can mislead without lying, for example by omitting to mention other important truths. There have even been scientists who manufactured their results in the belief that they were serving a higher truth, the one they already knew, or thought they did.

Perhaps, then, I was mistaken to linger over Maurizio Serra's first sentence. One can read carelessly, but perhaps also too closely.

Virginia Woolf's biography of Elizabeth Barrett Browning's dog, Flush, begins with a kind of elephantine pseudo-erudite facetiousness, which I suppose is the nearest the author could come to humour. For me, at any rate, the most interesting passage in the book is about the kidnapping of Flush by an East End gang who demanded a ransom for him. Elizabeth wanted to pay it (and did), while her father, brother and her future husband, Robert Browning, were against doing so. He who pays the Danegeld, after all, never gets rid of the Dane.[3]

The moral and psychological battle lines were drawn. The men in the story thought in abstractions while the woman thought in particularities. The men were against paying the ransom because, if ransoms were paid, more of them would be demanded and such crime would be encouraged. The woman, by contrast, thought only of her love for the dog, imagining his death if the ransom were not paid; and in a household in which love, or at least manifestations of love, were in short supply, her love for her dog counted for more than any mere abstraction could.

Let me say at once that if it were my dog that were kidnapped for ransom, I should unhesitatingly pay it, though with a slightly guilty conscience, for I should recognise the force of the opposing argument.

Woolf writes:

> Her father and her brother were in league against her and were capable of any treachery in the interest of their class.

But what class was that? Not social class, for Elizabeth Barrett, however unhappy she may have been, was of the same social class as they. Of the class of domineering fathers and brothers? But Robert Browning, her suitor, was of the same opinion. Of the class of men or males, then? But can it really be in the

---

[3] In actual fact, Flush *was* kidnapped — dognapped? — three times, a fact which Virginia Woolf omits, possibly for literary reasons but possibly for other reasons also.

interest of the class of males in general not to pay ransoms, while it is in the interest of females as a class to pay them? There is a refusal here to address the argument by ascribing malevolence to it, or at least self-interest (and who is free of self-interest?).

Woolf also says:

> Miss Barrett was not to be intimidated. Miss Barrett took up her pen and refuted Robert Browning… what would Mr Browning have done if the bandits had stolen her; had her in their power; threatened to cut off her ears and send them by post to New Cross [where he was living]?

The word here *refuted* is wrong. Woolf should have said 'Miss Barrett took up her pen and *argued against* Robert Browning,' for her argument, though a powerful one, was not a refutation. Powerful as it is, the argument would not in logic force Browning to change his mind. The analogy between Flush and Miss Browning is not exact; and in fact governments *do* sometimes have to decide whether or not to pay ransoms for kidnapped citizens (their practices may not accord with their declared principles).

What the word *refuted* implies is that there is an indubitably correct solution to the dilemma; but it is in the nature of the tragic dilemma that there should not be such. The use of the word refuses the tragic dimension of the situation, though it is obvious. No perfect outcome is envisageable. It would be terrible if the kidnappers of Flush should be rewarded for their crime; it would be terrible if Flush should be killed by them. A choice has to be made; but the encouragement of the kidnappers means that sorrow will inevitably be transferred to others.

As I have indicated, I am sympathetic to Elizabeth Barrett. At any rate, she decided to go to the kidnappers' lair, pay the ransom and recover Flush. This was a brave thing for a young woman brought up in upper middle-class London to have done. Woolf writes:

> She told Wilson [her maid] to call a cab. All trembling but submissive, Wilson obeyed. The cab came. Miss Barrett told Wilson to get in. Wilson, though convinced that death awaited her, got in.

Note that Wilson has no name other than Wilson, which reduces her almost to a function rather than a person. Moreover, Woolf does not find it at all remarkable that a servant can simply be ordered to confront a situation that she believes will be fatal to herself. In Doctor Johnson's *Rassselas*, the Princess of Abyssinia does *not* order her servant to confront her fear of death by forcing her to enter the narrow passage in the Great Pyramid, but instead assuages it by not insisting. When one reads of Woolf's attitude to servants, and to her social inferiors in general, it is not surprising that she fails to notice Elizabeth Barrett's high-handedness, because it was her own. Talk about the interest of their class!

Browsing among my books, which are so many that it is like browsing in quite a decent second-hand bookshop, I came across a volume of essays by the philosopher, Antony Flew, titled *A Rational Animal and other Philosophical Essays on the Nature of Man*.

I knew Flew slightly through another friend. At the time, he was still an atheist, indeed a militant one. It was he who argued that there should be a presumption against the existence of God and that it was up to deists to prove His existence in much the same way, I suppose, that it is up to the believers in the existence of the Loch Ness Monster to prove its existence, rather than up to sceptics to prove its non-existence. Towards the end of his long life, however, in his eighties, he publicly announced that he had become himself a deist, having been convinced by the argument from design. Although there were rumours that he had gone the whole hog, as it were, and converted to Christianity (his father had been a Methodist minister), he denied this, refusing to ascribe any particular qualities or characteristics to the deity in whose existence he now believed. The question was immediately raised after his conversion as to whether his change of mind on the question was the consequence of a decline into senility. I am uncertain whether this question has been settled beyond reasonable doubt, but that it was raised at all illustrates the speed with which discussions of a question — here, that of the existence of God — supposedly 'objective' or at least abstract, descend to the *ad hominem* which, of course, is always fun.

A Rational Animal was published in 1978, before the term *political correctness* was current or even coined. But in the prologue to the book, Flew glimpses the shape of things to come with what seems to be remarkable prescience, as I shall indicate.[4]

The final essay in the book is titled *Lenin and the Cartesian Inheritance*. This is a discussion of Lenin's implicit acceptance, in his one work of epistemology, *Materialism and Empirio-Criticism*, of Cartesian scepticism. (Even in matters of epistemology, Lenin manages to be bilious and rancorous.) In 1978, of course, Lenin was a figure to be taken much more seriously than he is now, for his legacy was still alive and few foresaw its imminent collapse and loss of prestige. In the prologue, Flew gives the history of this essay, which was first published in English and Serbo-Croat in Yugoslavia, then still a real entity though few appreciated just how fragile an entity. The journal in which it was published was called *Praxis*, headquartered in Zagreb. Flew continues:

> What makes it in its own way a special case is that that journal, after a career including much honourable conflict with state authorities, seems now to have been suppressed finally; although its Editorial Board, with the support of the Croatian Philosophical Association, refuses formally to disband.

And in a footnote to this, Flew writes what is particularly relevant to our present conjuncture:

---

[4] When I first wrote this sentence, I used the word *preface* rather than *prologue*. Then I checked it. This demonstrates how fallible memory — or perhaps I should say *my* memory — is, even in small matters when there appears to be nothing at stake. Not all error or every lapse of memory is motivated.

British readers, when they learn that this suppression was effected not by administrative order and official police action, but by exercise of 'workers' control', will be able, though too often reluctant, to recognise the sinister shape of things beginning to come… The explanation which the *Praxis* Editorial Board circulated to subscribers and friends included the sentence '… the printing house in which the Yugoslav edition of *Praxis* has been printed from its first issue sent us a notice saying that the political activists and the governing body of this Organization of Associated Work have taken the decision that in future the service of printing the journal *Praxis* should be discontinued.'

Exact repetition is not to be expected in history, but who can fail to notice the analogy with the monstrous regiment of *sensitivity readers* and other sniffers-out of heresy who now infest publishing houses, especially those with the greatest reach and resources?

Some short lines are piercing. Usually they are couched in very simple words. Among them is Gloucester's reply to the old man who says to him, after his eyes have been put out, 'You cannot see your way.'

'I have no way,' says Gloucester, 'and therefore want no eyes.'

Could despair go deeper or be expressed more simply? And yet the rhythm of the utterance is also attended to. A perfect line, then, that remains in the mind.

Another such line is Malvolio's departing curse or exclamation of impotent rage. Whatever it may be, it transforms him in a few words from a figure of fun into a tragic figure:

I'll be revenged on the whole pack of you.

Through these nine words, one realises the depths of the hurt and humiliation caused by the cruel jest played upon him by his social superiors who have failed completely to consider him as a feeling being. The fact that he is not an admirable person makes this sudden reversal of our attitude towards him, from disdain to sympathy, all the more startling. We suddenly see Malvolio as we had not seen him before, a wounded man, and as such we commiserate with him.

Perhaps I am especially sensitive to this line because I sometimes suspect that I am something of a Malvolio-figure myself: pompous, self-important, ridiculous, the object of mockery. Therefore, Malvolio makes me feel nervous, or at least insecure.

There is also a line in Ruskin's autobiography, *Praeterita* (The Bygone) that is similarly piercing. As is often the way with Victorian autobiographies, perhaps with most autobiographies, Ruskin describes the peculiarities of his upbringing. (All upbringings are peculiar in the sense of being unique, another factor limiting, thank goodness, the possibility of human uniformity.) Ruskin's father was a rich wine and sherry merchant, his mother very religious. He had a protected childhood, in some ways very privileged, in others highly constraining. When he went to Oxford, his mother accompanied him and installed herself in an inn in order to oversee him. It is not surprising that he suffered psychological problems throughout his life, though I write this with trepidation because the only real criterion of psychological explanation in a case like this is plausibility, which is a very loose criterion, everything and its opposite, and everything between them, being susceptible to rationalisation into plausibility.

Ruskin enumerates the advantages and disadvantages of his upbringing, starting with the former:

> The first and greatest of these was the perfect peace and harmony between my parents which resulted in an equally calm household: no raised voices, no disputes, no trivial crises, no hard words even to the servants. This calmness induced a habit of obedience [in Ruskin], for what was there to rebel against?

I doubt that anyone would now consider the inculcation of the habit of obedience as a benefit. We have long valued rebellion as a good in itself, almost irrespective of what is rebelled against, or even how it is rebelled against. As to the perfection of the peace of the Ruskin household, I am reminded of the joke in which a child, completely mute until the age of ten, causing his parents to believe that he is congenitally impaired, suddenly asks them at the dinner table to pass the salt. 'Why haven't you said anything before, since you can speak?' ask his astonished parents. 'Until now,' replies the child, 'everything has been perfect.'

The next blessing of his upbringing, Ruskin says, was 'an

extreme perfection in palate and all other bodily senses.' His father had taste and transferred or communicated it to his son. Ruskin, of course, became the foremost aesthetician of his time, and one of the most influential aestheticians of *any* time — though, alas, one can be influential without being right.

Then Ruskin enumerates the disadvantages of his upbringing. Here come the seven words that are made to stand as a paragraph on their own. He writes of the disadvantages:

First, that I had nothing to love.

Nothing — by which, surely, he also means nobody — to love: everything in his little world ran like clockwork. His parents were *correct* rather than loving. How terrible is a loveless world (I know, because I grew up in one)! And what suffering these few words convey! It cannot be said that lovelessness abrogates all other advantages, which may be genuine enough; but it causes many a subsequent difficulty and affects a person's subsequent stance towards the world such that, however outwardly normal he may appear, inwardly he retains a distance from the rest of humanity (not that Ruskin ever appeared outwardly normal).

Ruskin analyses with considerable finesse the consequences of his cold but correct upbringing:

The evil consequence of all this was not, however, what might perhaps have been expected, that I grew up selfish or unaffectionate; but that, when affection did come, it came with violence utterly rampant and unmanageable,

38

at least by me, who never before had anything to manage.

With the kind of genuine self-examination which it is the effect if not the intention of psychologists to render superfluous or even impossible, Ruskin goes on to say, with admirable objectivity:

> My present verdict, therefore, on the general tenor of my education at that time, must be, that it was at once too formal and too luxurious; leaving my character, at the most important moment for its construction, cramped indeed, but not disciplined; and only by protection innocent, instead of by practice virtuous.

I do not, of course, claim that self-examination of this excoriatingly truthful kind is the answer to all of life's problems: for nothing is *that*.

As I write this, the war in Ukraine continues. The city of Mariupol (of which, though it had a population of 450,000, I suspect that most people had never heard) is reported destroyed, the performance of the Russian army being so bad that mass destruction of cities is the only way that Mr Putin can win his war — as win he must, if he is to survive. My hope — at this very moment — is that someone in his entourage, either from moral conviction or from some other contorted motive, will assassinate him. It comes to this: war makes us rejoice in the death, actual or potential, of others.[5]

I recently gave a lecture, on-line, about H.G. Wells. Among my many books by him is a slender paperback, published by Penguin in 1943, titled *Crux Ansiata: An Indictment of the Roman Catholic Church*. (The *Crux Ansiata* is the handle-shaped cross, a symbol that pre-dated Christianity but was adopted as its own by the Coptic Church.) The book is cheaply produced, as one would expect in wartime, and carries advertisements on its covers that are not without interest in themselves. The first is for Mars bars, 'Sustaining, Energising, Nourishing,' but with this notice in small lettering:

> ZONING now restricts Mars to the Southern Counties. So here's hoping for quick victory – and plenty of Mars for everyone – everywhere.

In fact, the rationing in Britain of sweetstuffs lasted another six years, including four after the end of the war.

On the back cover is a stern-looking guardsman in a busby, presumably a colonel in the Royal Scots Greys, for the advertisement in which he appears is for Grey's Cigarettes, which he is more or less *ordering* the readers to smoke because they are 'Just honest-to-goodness tobacco'. Honest-to-goodness tobacco is a concept without application these days, all tobacco being bad, having been dishonestly promoted long after the harmful effects of smoking were known (including, of course, to smokers themselves). In 1943, people hardly needed to be encouraged to smoke. Not to do so was almost eccentric,

---

[5] Not that a successor would necessarily be better than Mr Putin.

as was leaving home without a hat. How everything in those days must have smelt of stale smoke: curtains, bedclothes, sofas, woollens, even walls and doors! Yet no one noticed or remarked on it, an example of mass sensory adaptation. Now even a single cigarette smoked at a distance of yards can make me cough.

Wells' little book of 96 pages, albeit closely-printed, is a romp through the history of Catholicism of the kind useful to village atheists (of whom I was once one). I suppose that most people who thought of a reason to 'indict' the Catholic Church in 1943 would think of its silence about the Holocaust, then at its climax, but Wells might not have known about it at the time and in any case was never well-disposed towards Jews, often indulging in the mild antisemitism common at the time.

What startles in the book is the vehemence of the author's hatred of Rome itself. I quote *in extenso* so that I shall not be thought to have torn a sentence out of context:

> On June 1st, 1942, the enemy bombed Canterbury and as near as possible, got the Archbishop of Canterbury. But what is a mere Protestant Archbishop against His Holiness the Pope?
>
> In March, 1943 Rome was still unbombed.
>
> Now consider the following facts.
>
> We are at war with the Kingdom of Italy, which made a particularly cruel and stupid attack upon our allies Greece and France; which is the homeland of Fascism; and whose "Duce" Mussolini begged particularly for the privilege of bombing London.

Wells here rather conveniently forgets that in 1932 he had called for an intelligent form of fascism in his own country and that he was never really a democrat, always believing that an enlightened elite should rule, and that this elite should self-consciously form itself rather than be formed informally or spontaneously, as elites are currently formed. His friend, George Bernard Shaw, never saw a totalitarian dictator whom he did not like. Wells continues:

> There are also Italian troops fighting against our allies the Russians. A thorough bombing (à la Berlin) of the Italian capital seems not only desirable but necessary. At present a common persuasion that Rome will be let off lightly by our bombers is leading to a great congestion of the worst elements of the Fascist order in and around Rome.

This is not the only reason that Rome should be bombed, in effect destroyed:

> Not only is Rome the source and centre of Fascism [again Wells forgets his former attraction to it], but it has been the seat of the Pope, who, as we shall show, has been an open ally of the Nazi-Fascist-Shinto Axis since his enthronement. He has never raised his voice against that Axis... and the pleas he is now making for peace and forgiveness are manifestly designed to assist the escape of these criminals...

On the last charge, Wells was not mistaken: there is abundant evidence that the Church was complicit in the exfiltration of war criminals to South America and elsewhere. But would that justify reducing St Peter's to rubble?

Wells cannot be accused of being mealy-mouthed. 'No other capital,' he says, 'has been spared the brunt of this war.' Actually, this is not quite true, but let it pass. '*Why* do we not bomb Rome?' asks Wells, and provides an answer that would justify a pogrom. 'The answer... opens up a very serious indictment of the mischievous social disintegration inherent in contemporary Roman Catholic activities.'

This little book should stand as a warning to all those who would write in the heat of the moment, in the fury of a passion, however understandable the latter might be. It is worth remembering also that Wells, in the very year of the Wright Brothers' first manned flight, 1903, predicted that manned flight would be used for military purposes, including the bombing and destruction of cities: a warning, not an endorsement. Forty years later he was advocating the obliteration by bombs of one of the great glories of human civilisation. How thin is the veneer of that civilization: all the more precious precisely because it is a veneer. What would life be without veneers?

Nasty, brutish and short.

That the most talented and prominent French novelist of his generation is also a pornographer is beyond dispute. He laces his books with repetitive descriptions of what are clearly his own sexual fantasies that neither advance the story – quite the reverse, in fact – or enhance the fundamental point that he is making with regard to sex, namely that in our times, thanks to the freedoms wrought in the 1960s (in France in May, 1968 in particular), we have become ever more incompetent in the matter of intimate relations, sex having become the mere satisfaction of a biological itch which must be scratched regularly, and not an expression of love. Perhaps because of his advancing age, the pornographic content of his latest and longest novel, *Anéantir* (Annihilate) is considerably reduced.

I have heard it said that Houellebecq includes his pornographic passages to increase his sales, but I do not believe it. I think he is a *sincere* pornographer.

Be that as it may, he is also the most brilliant observer known to me of tendencies in western society, with a wonderful capacity to distil modern absurdities and expose ideological pretensions (and their practical consequences) in a few words or in a short scene. In one of his books, for example, he described the job of a university teacher of economics as that of purveying obvious falsehoods to careerist cretins, the description being that of the teacher himself, thereby exposing the moral corruption that pervades our society and will continue to do so for the foreseeable future.

In another scene, he described the arrival of the protagonist's long-absent former girlfriend, who arrives from Japan with very expensive designer suitcases which do not have the vulgar little wheels that would render them easy to manoeuvre. Such luggage, says Houellebecq, would make sense in a country in which there were porters to carry it, but we have suppressed all such employment and pay the people who might have undertaken it to do nothing instead. Thus do we eliminate one of the small amenities of life.

In his latest book (latest, that is, as I write this), one of the main characters works in a department of state that has moved its offices into a modern office block of the kind that French architects believe to be in advance of their time, believing as they do in the Whig interpretation of architectural history:

> He had never found any particular aesthetic merit in this arbitrary juxtaposition of glass and steel, which dominated the sad, muddy landscape. In any case, the object of the designers was not beauty, not even praise, but rather the display of a certain technical ability – as if it were a matter of, above all, making that ability clear to extraterrestrials.

Could there be a better or more succinct summary of the activities of those now known as starchitects, such as Frank Gehry, Norman Foster, Jean Nouvel, Renzo Piano, Daniel Liebeskind, *et al.*, whom Houellebecq pins to the board as an entomologist pins a moth or a butterfly. They build not for humans, but for another species entirely, one as yet to be discovered, in short extraterrestrials. Fools, of course, can be found to praise their efforts, who are afraid to be thought unable to 'understand' them; and it is also true that our schools of architecture have taken on the task of converting young human beings into extraterrestrials, as colonial authorities once thought of converting natives into Englishmen or Frenchmen. It must be admitted that, in this task, they have succeeded brilliantly. Talking to an architectural critic who himself has undergone such a training is like talking to a Martian who has learned several elements of our language without any connection to their meaning and has never heard of *beauty* and never encountered any possible application of the concept.

In short, we have permitted architects to become extraterrestrials with an extraterrestrial sensibility (if that is quite the word for it).

Over and over again, Houellebecq displays this ability to distil in a few lines the deformations, maladies, pathologies and absurdities of our time.

Richard Baxter was the most eminent writer who ever lived in my small town, though he did not do so for long and thought the townsfolk a drunken, impious rabble. There are still a large number of pubs in the town, at least one per thousand inhabitants — the Bear, the Black Boy, the Golden Lion, the Shakespeare, the King's Head, the Crown, the Falcon, the Harp, to name but a few — within a few hundred yards of my house. Amazingly enough, they all have their own type of clientele, from late-stage alcoholics to young drug-dealers and takers to farming types with gun dogs.

My town is the kind in which the young seek stimulating drugs rather than tranquillising ones. Urban life in Britain may be divided metaphorically into two categories: that in which heroin is consumed, and that in which amphetamines are consumed.

Richard Baxter lived (for a year, 1640-41) four doors away from my house, in a small cottage which is now painted with the words 'In this house lived the learned and eloquent Richard Baxter', which for years I read as 'learned and elegant', preferring, I suppose, elegance to eloquence, a more deceiving quality, especially when united to religious belief, when it is so often tinged with insincerity, hypocrisy or even downright fraudulence.

Baxter, a semi-Puritan divine, wrote and published more words than almost any other writer in English, at least until the advent of Frank Richards, the creator of the immortal Billy Bunter, who is said to have written 100,000,000 words, and on occasion 35,000 a day. Knowing no more of Richard Baxter than what I had read in the *Dictionary of National Biography*, I rashly offered to give a talk on him to the local historical society, as a result of which offer, accepted with alacrity, I felt constrained to read a little — a very little — of what he had written. No library within reasonable distance stocking any of his works, not now much in demand, I ordered some cheap American reprints. It seems that only Americans of evangelical persuasion read him these days.

The reprints were nasty as physical artifacts, of course: evangelicals, on the whole, are not much concerned with the aesthetic aspects of human existence. I started with the slimmest of the volumes, titled *The Cure of Depression and Excessive Sorrow*, a kind of Prozac of the soul, though Baxter himself does not use the weasel word *depression*, but rather melancholy. It seems that even the evangelicals are sufficiently modern to replace it by the protean concept of depression, that is to say any deviation from a state of complete happiness, which as we know is the norm for Mankind.

The book outraged me very quickly — but not because of anything that Baxter wrote, quite the contrary. In certain respects, Baxter was far more realistic than modern psychiatrists and appreciates the necessity for and inevitability of judgment. He says:

> Sorrow is excessive when it is fed by a mistaken cause. All is too much where none is due, and great sorrow is too much when the cause required less.

The estimation of the degree of sorrow justified by circumstances cannot be exact, of course, and requires the kind of judgment that modern psychiatrists, with their checklist mentality, are increasingly unwilling to make preparatory to their prescriptions. Baxter was more sophisticated and had a better grasp of human reality. He continues:

> If a man thinketh that somewhat a duty, which is no duty, and then sorrow for omitting it, such sorrow is all too much, because it is undue, and caused by error.

Excessive guilt is one of the symptoms of melancholia, that rare but serious form of depression that is now subsumed by the term depression, that often trivial lowering of mood that afflicts multitudes (if not everyone) at some time. Baxter goes on to describe a state of mind that is by no means alien to the militantly secular, who imagine themselves free of all the mental encumbrances of religion:

> Many fearful Christians are troubled about every meal that they eat, about their clothes, their thoughts, and words, thinking that all is sinful which is lawful, and that

unavoidable infirmities are heinous sins… The passions of grief and trouble of mind do oft overthrow the sober and sound use of reason, so that a man's judgment is corrupted and perverted by it, and is not in that case to be trusted.

No doubt we can all think of instances of this, though we should not always agree as to when it applies.

Why did the book outrage me, though? It was because the editors and publishers replaced Baxter's scriptural quotations, taken from the Authorised or Kings James Version, and replaced them by something called the *English Standard Version*, 'copyright 2002 by Crossway, a publishing ministry of Good News Publishers.' The ESV is a registered Trade Mark, and 'Unauthorised reproduction of the publication is prohibited' and 'all rights reserved'. Not such good news after all.

Almost needless to say, the English Standard Version has all the verbal grandeur of a bus timetable. By contrast, the language of the Authorised or King James Version is so beautiful, at least for a native speaker of English, that it gives even the most hardened atheist something of a will to believe.

The argument in favour of the use of a modernised version is, I suppose, that it is more readily comprehensible to the average person, who should not be put to any unnecessary effort to understand. This is an odd argument to use in the context of a seventeenth century text that has not otherwise been modernised; and the fact remains that modern versions of the Bible are quite without literary merit or beauty of language. For latterday Puritans, no doubt, who think only of content or doctrine, and not of form, the lack of literary beauty is itself a virtue, since it purifies rather than distracts the mind, though it also has the disadvantage of making inconsistency all the more evident. I feel nothing but contempt for this suburbanisation of language (the Authorised or King James Version was not ordinary language even in its day).

When, as sometimes I do, I seek a Biblical quotation on the internet, several modern versions appear before that of 1611, all of which I find snivelling. Here is a little of the Sermon on the Mount in a modern version (in this case, not the English Standard Version):

> And why worry about your clothing? Look at the lilies of the field and how they grow. They don't work or make their clothing, yet Solomon in all his glory was not dressed as beautifully as they are. And if God cares so wonderfully for wildflowers, that are here today and thrown into the fire tomorrow, he will certainly care for you. Why do you have so little faith?

Compare this with:

> And why take ye thought for raiment? Consider the lilies of the field, how they grow; they toil not, neither do they spin. And yet I say unto you, That even Solomon in all his glory was not arrayed like one of these. Wherefore, if God so clothe the grass of the field, which today is, and tomorrow is cast into the oven, shall he not much more clothe you, O ye of little faith.

And 'Sufficient unto the day is the evil thereof' becomes

'Today's trouble is enough for today.' Class dismissed.

The new versions of the Bible are as much an improvement on the old as Frank Gehry is on Palladio.

My formal literary education ceased when I was fifteen, and I have received no more since. It has not been my observation, however, that everyone who studies literature in a formal fashion loves it, quite the contrary. Their studies have the effect on them that Scotch had on me when I was nineteen. I once drank far too much of it (in order to prove my adulthood) and have never been able to abide it in the more than half a century since.

I was fortunate, however, that my last lesson in literature was given by a woman of pedagogical talent (which I have not), who brought us to appreciate the poems of Gerard Manley Hopkins. I do not remember how she did it, except that her method was Socratic, and she drew the meaning of the poems out of us, so to speak. I wish now that I had expressed my gratitude to her at the time, but such is not the way of youth, especially youth that is half-pleased with, half-unsure of, itself. There was a time when I wanted to be a teacher, but besides having no gift for pedagogy, I would have been afraid that my pupils[6] would have surpassed me in achievement, and *that* I should have found it difficult to tolerate.

---

[6] Like the word *unhappy* (replaced by the word *depressed*), the word *pupil* has almost disappeared from our lexicon in favour of *student*, which is felt to be more respectful of children. However, it infantilises students more than it matures children.

Hopkins, of course, was a religious poet, but I do not recall what my teacher's religious views were, or even if she had any, for in those days teachers steered clear of religion, politics and sex, partly as a matter of duty and partly as a matter of taste. They approached much by indirection, and on the whole I think it was better so. Still, one could hardly miss the religious impulse (aspect would be too weak a word) of Hopkins' poetry. In his case, the AMDG (*Ad maiorem Dei gloriam*), the mission statement of the Society of Jesus of which he was a member, that he affixed to his work, was no mere figure of speech. And the strange thing is that, though I did not believe in God, I knew what he meant, and such is his poetry that I wished I could share his belief, just as I do if I read the Psalms. But still I don't.

When Hopkins says 'The world is charged with the grandeur of God,' one understands how he has come to this conclusion, and respects it. 'As kingfishers catch fire, dragonflies draw flame': who, on seeing such things, doesn't give thanks for his existence, indeed for existence in general? There might have been nothing rather than something, and therefore, surveying all that there is, we come to the view, or feeling, that existence itself is good, forgetting its evils. I think of Hopkins when I see a finch's wings (alas more rarely these days):

> All thinks counter, original, spare, strange;
> Whatever is fickle, freckled (who knows how?)
> With swift, slow, sweet, sour; adazzle, dim;
> He fathers-forth whose beauty is past change:
> Praise him.

When one sees a field of poppies, a grove of bluebells in a wood, the twitching whiskers of a mouse, who cannot think of a benevolent creator who has set all this in motion and arranged this for us?

Do those of religious sensibility appreciate the beauty of the world more than the irreligious? That Hopkins' response to the beauty of the world is profound and sincere is not in doubt: here is none of the soapiness than can afflict the religious, or rather embarrass their interlocutors. But are the religious more susceptible to beauty than atheists? Consider the poem by A.E. Housman, written more or less at the same time as Hopkins' above quoted, Housman having been an atheist who lost his faith on the death of his beloved mother when he was twelve years old:

> Loveliest of trees, the cherry now
> Is hung with bloom along the bough,
> And stands about the woodland ride
> Wearing white for Eastertide.
>
> Now, of my threescore years and ten,
> Twenty will not come again,
> And take from seventy spring a score,
> It only leaves me fifty more.
>
> And since to look at things in bloom
> Fifty springs are little room,
> About the woodlands I will go
> To see the cherry hung with snow.

Is not the sincerity of this as evident as that of Hopkins' poem? And is not the fleetingness of life and the finality of death as good a reason to appreciate the world in the here and now as is its supposed creation by an all-wise, all-beneficent, all-powerful being?

Then, of course, there is the central problem of theodicy: the reconciliation of the perfect goodness of God with the existence, indeed prevalence, of evil, to which one might add ugliness. In his poem, *Pied beauty*, Hopkins hints at the necessity of contrast for us to be able to appreciate anything: but exactly how much evil is necessary for us to be able to appreciate goodness? Surely it should be the minimum necessary, which at the moment — and perhaps at every moment in history — it appears not to be.

The world does not reveal to us an indubitable meaning. Housman's 'blue remembered hills' caused him to reflect on the irreversibility, the irrecoverability of time, the happy highways where he went and could not go again. For Hopkins, 'the azurous hung hills' are God's 'world-wielding shoulder, majestic'. Do we derive our philosophy from the world, or the world from our philosophy?

Not that Hopkins was without his doubts. In his poem about the depths of misery available to the human mind, 'no worst, there is none,' he ends by refusing all consolation such as a belief in a happy after-life might be expected to confer:

> Here! creep,
> Wretch, under a comfort serves in a whirlwind: all
> Life death does end and each day dies with sleep.

We wake from sleep, but not from death.

In Britain in the decades before the First World War, and especially between the wars, certain eminent barristers, above all those for the defence in highly-publicised criminal cases, were as film-stars today, the object of adulation (but much more interesting). I had an aunt who uttered the words *Queens Counsel* (Q.C.) with almost religious awe composed of the deepest respect and admiration. She had grown up in an era when the names of the greatest advocates were household words, men such as Rufus Isaacs, Marshall Hall, Edward Carson, Henry Curtis-Bennett, Patrick Hastings, Norman Birkett, J.D. Cassels, and others.

It came to pass that her only son, a wayward boy, my first cousin, once needed defending in court against a serious criminal charge, including the illegal possession of a gun. He was undoubtedly guilty, and was found guilty, but his Q.C. pleaded with eloquence and he was given only a suspended sentence: which turned out to have been a wise disposal on the part of the judge, for my cousin turned Buddhist (like the famous barrister and judge, Christmas Humphreys, son of the famous barrister and judge, Travers Humphreys, but who nevertheless felt no qualms about passing the sentence of death) and became a very successful, and honest, businessman. My aunt was forever grateful to her son's Q.C., whose advocacy only increased her reverence for the tribe, which I myself partly feel.

Among my favourite reading are the memoirs or biographies of the famous advocates of the golden age, when the public, as a form of entertainment, still read the transcripts of trials with avidity. No doubt this was prurient, but it was intelligent prurience that required concentration for its satisfaction. Recently I read *The Life of Patrick Hastings* by his daughter, Patricia Hastings. In her acknowledgements, she writes, 'Most of all, I thank my mother to whom I dedicate this book, in spite of the fact that she has no intention of reading it.'

This sounds rather barbed in what was once a typically English way, a compliment and a criticism at the same time, a condensed expression of both love and conflict or clash of personality. The book was published in 1959, on the cusp of the mirror-image change in the English character, from indirection and subtlety to coarseness and literal-mindedness: in short, much less interesting.

The title page of the book states that it comes 'With a preface by Viscount Monckton of Brenchley'. This was the last gasp of British respect for titles, which no doubt was always absurd, considered in the abstract, and in many respects harmful, but which yet gave a savour to social life that has since been lost. Even now, someone like Mr Blair, a supposed tribune of 'the many, not the few', accepts a title, while of course wanting still to be known by the diminutive of his first name, thus turning himself into a mixed metaphor made flesh.

Monckton, a lawyer and politician, must have been one of the last men to be given an hereditary peerage. He had wanted to be Lord Chief Justice, but (among other things) became chairman of the Midland Bank instead. He was a man of integrity: he opposed the Suez adventure, and his preface to Patricia Hastings' book was not absurdly fulsome. On the contrary, the modesty of the claims it makes for the book speak to their honesty, an honesty that would be rare today and in a way is a compliment to the public of the day that did not demand incontinent superlatives:

> This book is a work of filial piety and affectionately written. Even if it cannot in the nature of things be the critical appreciation of the great advocate... it is a vivid account of a most interesting personality with faults and foibles but outstanding qualities.

I doubt that a publisher today would welcome so lukewarm (but accurate) an encomium to a book that it proposed to publish.

Hastings' father was a charming confidence trickster who, when he was in funds, lived in luxury and on a grand scale; but his periods of prosperity, always founded upon fraud or near-fraud, were brief, poverty soon following. Hastings' home life was thus very unstable, an alternation of the Savoy and cheap lodgings. Patricia Hastings says of her paternal grandfather:

> He had played cricket for the school and distinguished himself in the classics, for he possessed a remarkably good memory and was able to quote at length passages from Virgil and Homer. On the strength of these early triumphs he walked superbly though his life, somewhat surprised by the series of failures of all his many enterprises. I can't imagine why so many influential people seem to have fallen in with his plans, but perhaps

it was because he appears to have made a practice of doing things in a big way.

This is highly reminiscent of a recent British Prime Minister. Of course, no analogy is exact (which is why it is an analogy rather than a copy or a repetition): Hastings' father was always 'impeccably dressed in frock-coat and top-hat', while the recent Prime Minister to whom I have referred looked, almost as a matter of principle, as if he had just escaped down a drainpipe having quickly dressed at the threatened denouement of an illicit love affair.

Hastings' last great case was the libel case brought by Professor Harold Laski against several newspapers. Laski was at the time chairman of the Labour Party, and Hastings had been attorney-general in the first Labour government, but the political connection or sympathy between the two men did not prevent Hastings from destroying Laski in cross-examination. At the end of the trial before the Lord Chief Justice, Lord Goddard, the judge said something which would sound pretty hollow in our day:

> … it is the birthright of Englishmen to say what they like, to write what they like, to write fearlessly and to write openly…

If this was ever true, it is certainly true no longer. We have become great watchers of our ps and qs.

In an introduction to a volume of stories by Stefan Zweig,

published in 1981, the novelist John Fowles tries to explain the neglect of this author in Britain, the country of which, after all, he was a citizen when he died. And it is certainly very striking how, when one crosses the Channel to France, one finds his books everywhere available. Every station bookstall has them, and they must have sold by the million. One ought not to conclude from this, however, that they are trashy or trivial, in the way that the works of D.. B.... are trashy or trivial.

In Germany, so I was told by a German lady of literary tastes, Zweig is not highly regarded. He is to German letters what Somerset Maugham is to English, and to admit to a liking for or admiration of Zweig is to lose caste. This is curious, for he was once one of the most highly regarded (and highest paid) authors in the world.

He was born in 1888 into a rich, cultivated and assimilated Jewish family in Vienna. He was cosmopolitan, with a particular love of France. His ideal was of a Europe, if not of a world, without borders. His novellas — he wrote only one full-length novel, *Beware of Pity*, a brilliant dissection of the dangers of falsified or exaggerated emotion, very salutary today — deal with the overmastering passions of Man (in which category I include women). In this, they resemble the stories of Maugham very closely.

Fowles suggests that a reason for Zweig's eclipse in the English-speaking world is that, when Nazism first grew in, and then took over, the German-speaking world, Zweig had been neither prescient nor strident enough in his denunciation of it. He had been tried by circumstances and found wanting (unlike, say, his great contemporary, Thomas Mann).

For example — and Fowles recounts this story — Zweig had written a libretto for an opera by the composer Richard Strauss just before Hitler took over. By the time the opera was ready for performance, Hitler was Chancellor. Strauss, decently in the circumstances, insisted that Zweig's name appeared as librettist, though as a Jew he was known to be anathema to the Nazis, and temporary permission was granted. According to his detractors, Zweig himself should have declined to have his work performed in Nazi Germany: it was weak of him to allow the performance to go ahead.

Against this, two defences might be urged. The first is that the performance might have gone ahead anyway but with his name removed, for the Nazis were hardly sticklers for legal niceties in such matters; and the second, that a performance of an opera by the greatest German composer of the time with a libretto by a Jewish author might go to demonstrate the absurdity of Nazi antisemitism.

But the fact remains that Zweig never publicly denounced Nazism until he committed suicide in Brazil in 1942 (which Mann, less than generously, thought was a dereliction of duty on Zweig's part). Against this, too, might be urged two considerations. First, his denunciation would have been pointless, it would have done no good, and would besides have been entirely superfluous: for who could have supposed that Zweig, driven into exile from his beloved homeland, was anything *other* than deeply anti-Nazi? Even to suggest this would have been an insult.

Second, Zweig did not want any political situation, however dire or horrible, to determine what he had to say. To have denounced Nazism would have been to grant it too much credit, as if it stood in need of refutation. The Viennese satirist Karl Kraus said that when it came to Hitler, he couldn't think of anything to say — this from a man who wrote millions and millions of words. Zweig was probably of the same mind: if you feel you have to *denounce* Hitler, you are granting him an intellectual significance that he did not have.

This was probably wrong, a mistake, but one can understand it. And in fact, Zweig did much charitable work to assist less fortunately placed refugees than himself, though in an unobtrusive or inconspicuous way.

I think Fowles misses an important reason for the neglect of Zweig in England and his less than brilliant reputation in Germany: he was so intensely readable. When once you start to read Zweig, you always want to read straight through to the end, to know the denouement: you turn the pages eagerly, without effort. This intense readability did not come about by accident. Zweig would pare down his first draft of a story by two thirds, leaving only the essentials. No author known to me was so ruthless with his own first or second thoughts, with the result that his stories are lean, without descriptive fat, though he was nevertheless able (as was Maugham) to conjure up an atmosphere, or capture a scene, in a couple of lines.

But for all his simplicity, he was not trivial, unless human passion be trivial. No one is better able than he to convey the force of passion in human affairs. It is this combination of readability and non-triviality that is so unforgivable for those who think that literature should be a secret garden for initiates, or rather a jungle to be hacked through with the machetes of exegesis.

I know of few greater pleasures than to receive a book through the post unexpectedly, though I am aware that some people might think that this goes to show the crabbed and limited nature of my life. I report only what is the case.

Returning home from a three-day excursion to Wales, I found two books, neither of them expected, waiting for me. The first was *Brainspotting: Adventures in Neurology* by Professor Andrew Lees, one of the most eminent neurologists in the country, its greatest expert on Parkinson's disease. He kindly inscribed his book for me.

Many books that I read leave me with a feeling of shame, not very focussed or intense, but like a faint mist covering the landscape. I feel it because the author is my superior, either intellectually or morally, or both, and so it was with this short book, the autobiographical essays of a brilliant and humane neurologist.[7] I felt, and feel, his inferior both intellectually and morally because I have never been able to muster the intense concentration to master any field or make any positive scientific contribution, having too grasshoppery a mind to do so, being too readily distracted by the next thing that catches my interest or glitters on my mental horizon. Professor Lees has stuck to his medical last in order to bring far more comfort to his patients than I ever did; and, as if this were not all enough, he shows in this short book — shows, not displays — a literary erudition and sensibility into the bargain. He unites in himself the qualities of a scientist and an artist. He believes

---

[7] Neurologists as a tribe used to be thought of as the cold fishes of clinical medicine, cerebral without feeling, perhaps because they diagnosed without much hope of therapy.

in, and has contributed to, medical advance, but does not lose sight of the persisting need for humanity in the doctor's dealings with patients. There is a clear and present danger of the doctor becoming a mere technician or, worse still, bureaucrat.

Lees strikes me as a member of a species long thought to be extinct, the Renaissance man. It is not merely that nothing human is alien to him, but rather than *nothing* is alien to him. His curiosity is universal but not, like mine, idle.

In his book, he alludes without the stridency that comes naturally to me to the increasing managerialism of medicine as a human enterprise. This tendency seems to be like a natural force, as unstoppable as a volcanic eruption or tsunami, though more creeping and less dramatic, and though it comes about by human agency. Institutions with a distinguished, even glorious, history are closed down without a moment's hesitation or backward glance, let alone regret, on the basis of a reduced and probably spurious utilitarian calculation, but really because such institutions engage the loyalty of staff, and staff loyal to an institution are more difficult to manage or manipulate than those who are merely birds of passage who happen to draw their salary in one place rather than another.

In the book are clinical stories that remind me of my own little and much less distinguished career. Professor Lees had a patient, a Polish man in his early forties, who developed symptoms of Parkinson's disease, unusual at such an age. Lees treated him in conventional fashion, and he improved as expected. But the man's girlfriend told the patient to ask at the second consultation whether the Chinese herbal medicine that he was taking for stress and high blood pressure could have anything to do with his Parkinson's disease. Further investigation established that it did, and the man thus narrowly missed being diagnosed with a chronic and deteriorating condition for which he would have had to take powerful medication with serious side-effects for the rest of his life.

People are inclined to believe — *some* people, of course I mean — that herbal medicine, being 'natural', can do no harm, as if Nature were benevolently disposed to us. And I recall that once we had a patient who had heard that foxglove was good for the heart, who therefore made tea from a foxglove in her garden and promptly suffered from digitalis poisoning.

Likewise, non-western medicine is often assumed to be harmless at worst, but we had a few patients who were poisoned with lead, and in one case arsenic, from supposedly Ayurvedic medicine.

I think Lees would have liked our story of a man with lead poisoning whom we came to believe was poisoning himself with lead. He would come to hospital with a high level of lead in his blood which would then decline, but he would soon return with higher levels than ever. This alternation recurred over a prolonged period until we plucked up the courage to confront him with our conclusion. We did so, however, is such a way as to offer him an honourable way out. We told him that there were only three possible explanations of the pattern of his poisoning: that he was taking lead himself, that someone close to him was administering it to him, or that he was not drinking enough water.

'Yes, that must be it,' he said at once, though of course it was a completely bogus explanation. 'I never drink much water.'

A direct accusation would have been disastrous. Everyone needs an honourable way out at some time in his life.

Lees is my ideal as a doctor: learned, scientific, educated, cultivated and humane. From an early age he was highly observant of everything around him (he has a proper appreciation of the genius of Conan Doyle), and he was a disciplined and appreciative bird-watcher. He writes in a disarmingly lapidary style:

> Before I went to the London Hospital Medical College in Whitechapel, I had never seen a corpse. Death was hidden in our family and was something that happened to birds and old people.

The second book that awaited me on our return from our trip to Wales was a present from Mr Robert Downie, the founder-owner of Cosmos Books in Wem, Shropshire. Mr Downie has an unusual business: having been a bookseller since the age of sixteen, he saw an opportunity for a new type of business, namely the selling of individual articles from 18th and 19th century magazines.[8]

---

[8] I asked him whether he had qualms about breaking up volumes two centuries old. He did not, for a simple reason: these volumes, of no enormous rarity or aesthetic distinction, had gone unread for more than a century. By breaking them up, he was bringing the

By the time his premises were burnt down in an arson attack, presumably by a gang of drug dealers who were aiming at another such gang who had recently rented the premises next to his, he had catalogued 170,000 items, practically all burnt to a cinder: a quarter of a century's work gone up in smoke in the space of an hour or two. Over the years, I had bought quite a number of items from him, but I had never met him until after the fire, when I went to see him. Remarkably, he was not utterly downcast. This was despite the fact that the police, as alas we have now come to expect of them, failed completely to investigate the crime, let alone catch the criminals, and failed even to interview Mr Downie about any information he might have about the crime: but instead of ruminating on the various wrongs done him (the landlord, for example, having failed to take any notice of his tenants' evident criminality), he picked himself up and started again, finding new premises and new stock. Three months after the fire, his business was flourishing again. When I visited him, he said something that has stuck in my mind, so contrary was it to the temper of the times, with its emphasis on victimisation (it was admirable too). 'I've been victimised once,' he said. 'I'm not going to victimise myself a second time by spending my time complaining.'

I wrote a laudatory article about him for the *City Journal* of

---

attention of people like myself to articles that might interest them and of whose existence they would otherwise be unaware, but who did not want to encumber themselves with entire volumes, most of whose contents would not interest them. The fate of the volumes, sooner or later, would otherwise have been the dustheap. He was thus preserving rather than destroying.

New York. I thought that what he said had important lessons for psychology.

One small and beautifully bound book had, by some miracle, escaped the conflagration, the second edition of the *Poetry of the Anti-Jacobin*, published in 1854. This was the second book I received in the post, a present from Mr Downie. The binding was by Alfred de Sauty, one of the foremost bookbinders of the first years of the twentieth century. A little slip from a bookseller's catalogue dated March 1921, describes it thus: Plates by Gilray, green crushed levant morocco extra, t.e.g., gilt and blind tooled panels on side, with pellets in red, by De Sauty. (t.e.g. is a bookseller's acronym for top edge gilt. To every profession its acronyms. In medicine, T.E.G. stands for thromboelastography.)

The Anti-Jacobin was a weekly journal founded in 1797 by George Canning to counter pro-French revolutionary writing. Canning, whose dates of birth and death I can remember because they are the same as Beethoven's, was later to become Prime Minister, though he held office for a shorter time than any other British Prime Minister, his term of office cut short by death from natural causes.

The journal lasted for less than a year but was highly influential on the anti-revolutionary, conservative side. What is striking when one reads the journal's prospectus is how similar are the arguments employed to those of today. The so-called culture wars of the present are not very different from those of two and a quarter centuries ago:

In MORALS [says the prospectus] we are... old-fashioned. We have not yet learned the modern refinement of referring all considerations upon human conduct, not to any settled and preconceived principles of right and wrong, not to any general and fundamental rules which experience, and wisdom, and justice, and the common consent of mankind have established, but to the internal admonitions of every man's judgment or conscience in his own particular instance.

What, then, I had taken to be a modern state of mind, that no moral principle or rule of conduct is to be accepted without the person's consent or his having deduced it from a supposedly indubitable first principle, is not modern at all, but a strain of thought dating back at least to the time of *The Anti-Jacobin*. The prospectus continues:

We do not subscribe to the opinions, that a sincere conviction of the truth of no matter what principle, is a sufficient defence of no matter what action; and that the only business of moral enquiry with human conduct is to ascertain that in each case the principle and action agree.

That the doctrine complained of is no figment of a paranoid imagination is suggested by recent cases in which citizens who beyond doubt committed criminal actions have been acquitted because they were sincere in the beliefs that motivated them, or allegedly motivated them. (The impurity of human motivation does not unduly bother those who believe that sincerity of belief is an exculpation.)

George Canning, later Prime Minister, was a talented versifier. I have by heart two of his lines:

> In matters of commerce, the fault of the Dutch
> Is giving too little and asking too much.

The final edition of *The Anti-Jacobin* was devoted to a long poem, *New Morality*. It is clearly a forerunner to A.H. Clough's more famous *The Latest Decalogue* ('Thou shalt not kill; but needst not strive/ Officiously to keep alive' — often quoted in defence of euthanasia or assisted suicide, when the author was precisely defending, by means of satire, the sanctity of human life.)

Canning's poem satirised the tendency, now very prevalent, to locate moral concern in broad abstraction rather than in the immediate world around us:

> First, stern PHILANTHROPY – not she, who dries
> The orphan's tears, and wipes the widow's eye;
> Not she, who sainted Charity her guide,
> Of British bounty ours the annual tide: -
> But French Philanthropy; - whose boundless mind
> Grows with the general love of all mankind; -
> Philanthropy, - beneath whose baneful sway
> Each patriot passion sinks, and dies away.

The division between those who see morality and moral action as principally personal, and those who see it as principally social, legal and economic, exists still: and, as usually, there is something to be said on both sides, which are in perpetually unstable equilibrium. Canning, however, brilliantly satirises the *soi-disant* citizen of the world, the person who claims to belong nowhere and everywhere at the same time:

> No narrow bigot *he*; his reason'd view
> Thy interests, England, rank with those of Peru![9]
> France at our doors, *he* sees no danger nigh,
> But heaves for Turkey's woes th'impartial sigh;
> A steady patriot of the world alone,
> The friend of every country – but his own.

A passage from *The New Morality* is almost prophetic about the Russian Revolution more than a century later:

> JUSTICE, whose blood-stain'd book one sole decree,
> One statue, fills – "the People shall be Free!"
> Free! By what means? – by folly, madness, guilt,
> By boundless rapine, blood in oceans spilt;
> By confiscation, in whose sweeping toils
> The poor man's pittance with the rich man's spoils,
> Mix'd in one common mass, are swept away,
> To glut the short-lived tyrant of the day:
> By laws, religion, morals, all o'erthrown:
> Rouse then, ye sovereign people, claim your own:
> The licence that enthrals, the truth that blinds,
> The wealth that starves you, and the power that grinds!

Canning was not a blind reactionary, claiming the perfection of all that already existed. He admitted even great imperfections. But unlike lovers of humanity in general,

---

[9] A reference, surely, to Samuel Johnson's most famous poem, *The Vanity of Human Wishes*:
> Let observation with extensive view,
> Survey Mankind, from China to Peru…

Canning (in his Prospectus of the journal) hints at the necessity of aligning thought, policy and feeling:

> We have not so far gotten to the bottom of the influence of long habits and early education… but we have our feelings, our preferences, and our affection, attaching on particular places, manners, and institutions, and even on particular portions of the human race.

On the day on which I read this, I also read an article in the *Sunday Times* tut-tutting about Europe's generosity towards Ukrainian refugees and its comparative reticence about African or Syrian ones.

I returned in my mind to Professor Lees' book the night after reading it, when for some reason or other I could not sleep for an hour or two.

I was deeply impressed by one of the professor's teaching methods: he would take his students on the London Underground's Circle Line (which takes about an hour to complete) and tell them to observe the passengers with medical conditions, asking them to describe them in such a way that they could be identified by the person to whom they gave the description. This is a method reminiscent of that employed by Flaubert (the son of a doctor) in his teaching Maupassant to write. It sharpens the powers both of observation and description. 'You see but you do not observe,' said Holmes to Watson. 'You speak but you do not describe,' might be said of many of us.

Lees taught his students never to stop observing, which is all too easy for doctors to do. Their observations are framed by their expectations, as it were: in the clinic, they see clinical signs, but not elsewhere, though they abound. I had a personal experience of this half a century ago. As a young doctor, I frequented endocrinologists in the course of my professional duties, but they did not notice that I was grossly myxoedematous, that is to say thyroid-deficient. When I look at photographs of myself from that period (not that I do so often), I see an absolutely textbook case: I could have been an illustration in a textbook dating from 1880, before there was treatment for the deficiency. No trace of thyroid hormone was detectable in my blood; if I had suffered a mild viral illness, I might have slipped into a coma from which I would not have emerged. When, quite by chance, my condition was diagnosed (I had volunteered for an experiment in which one of the measurements was of Thyroid Stimulating Hormone), the professor brought his students to observe the slow relaxation phase of my ankle jerk reflex, a classical sign of severe thyroid deficiency, now rarely seen, and never with such clarity. If mobile telephones had existed in those days, my ankle jerk might have been immortalised for teaching purposes. It was thought a great joke at the time that a doctor should be such excellent teaching material.

If all the doctors around me had been taught by Professor Lees, my condition would have been diagnosed much the sooner.

Another manifestation of Professor Lees' independence of mind is his belief that the kind of clinical research now sanctioned by the medical establishment is too narrow and thereby misses possible advances. Double-blind trials are not, or ought not to be, the be-all and end-all of such research — though they have their place.

As a person whose only positive contribution to medical science was the recognition of a previously undescribed side-effect of an antimalarial drug, I am perhaps not in a strong position to comment. But I once thought that I had recognised a new syndrome, and had I had the energy and drive to write up a series of cases, it might usefully have entered medical nosology.

I noticed that certain persons in their late twenties or early- to mid-thirties would give up their work and withdraw from life. My first patient of this type (whose condition I recognised) was a high-flying banker who, over a matter of weeks or months, became increasingly silent and reclusive, until she holed herself up in her house and would very seldom leave. It was assumed by every doctor that she was severely depressed, but all the usual treatments for depression failed to work. She attended my clinic with her mother, who described a marked change in her daughter's character and conduct. Normally extrovert, talkative, and notably self-confident, she had become introverted and taciturn.

'And how does she spend her days?' I asked.

'She spends her days staring at the walls in a darkened room.'

'How darkened?'

'She draws the curtains in the middle of the day.'

This piece of information, that the patient had never given me herself, was a kind of key to the lock of her mind. She drew the curtains because she felt that people were looking at her, laughing or talking about her. She was not hallucinated or deluded, however; she merely felt that they were looking or laughing at her. These were ideas of reference, but she was not fully psychotic. Despite the relative mildness of these symptoms, they were having a devastating effect upon her life.

I prescribed a very tiny dose of anti-psychotic medication called trifluoperazine, very old-fashioned (and cheap), an excellent drug apart from one serious occasional side-effect, which fortunately my patient never experienced.

A week later, she was transformed: or rather, had returned to normal. She no longer hid herself away, was her outgoing self again and had resumed work. Her mother thanked me for not having written her off as a weak or worthless person. After all, doctors often blame failure on their patients.

I subsequently saw quite a few such patients, more women than men. I had no explanation of the pattern, but they all did well with very little treatment — without which, however, their lives remained deeply circumscribed or impaired.

I should have written the series up. If my observation was a true one, it was important. The pretext for my inertia was that medical journals these days are uninterested in case studies, fixated as they are on the double-blind study or vast epidemiological enquiries that require a vast statistical apparatus (that not one in a thousand doctors understands) for a meaning to be extracted from them. But still this was just a pretext that would not have deterred Professor Lees. My life has been one long lost opportunity.

When I started to write book reviews for publication, I thought it would be fun to write slashing reviews of bad books, but I soon matured from this idea to the rather gentler delight of finding errors in the text. Even this pleasure, however, soon palled: the recollection of my own numerous errors made me more tolerant of those of others. But I would not be quite truthful if I did not admit that pleasure in the discovery of error has altogether disappeared, competing with the pleasure of acquiring new knowledge. Every reviewer of books, I suspect, has an inner pedant waiting to be fed.

Having undertaken to write a short article about Virginia Woolf in a monthly magazine's series called *Sacred Cows*, I happened on a book in a Parisian bookshop with the title *Freud à Bloomsbury* by a practising psychoanalyst called Henriette Michaud, also student of English culture and literature. The book's subject is the *Standard Edition* of Freud's works in English, regarded as the most complete edition of his work in any language, edited and largely translated by James Strachey and his wife Alix. James was Lytton Strachey's brother, who was of course a major figure in the Bloomsbury set, and the book quotes Virginia Woolf many times (my excuse for having bought it). Imagine my delight as a pedant when I came across the following:

> The couple [James and Alix Strachey] hosted the Cambridge Fabians, who named themselves after the Roman Emperor Fabius and advocated a pacifist socialism, egalitarian between men and women, ascetic and atheist.

But Quintus Fabius Maximus Verrucosus was never Emperor,

only temporary Dictator (the first Roman emperor did not accede to the throne until two centuries later). Nor did the author allude to the very characteristic of Fabius's career that caused the group to name itself after him: that he did not confront the enemy (the Carthaginians under Hannibal) head-on, but rather harried and sapped it by constant little attacks until its strength gave out and it could resist no more. The Fabian socialists hoped that, by constant propaganda and gradual reforms and measures, they would achieve their end, socialism, thus avoiding a violent show-down such as a revolution. In other words, the author misses the essential.

The principal Fabians (not all) were of upper-middle class origin, and this may have been another reason for calling themselves after Fabius, who was also known as *Cunctator*, the Delayer. Without resorting to psychoanalysis, might one not find this revealing? Might they not have been the secular equivalents of St. Augustine, who prayed for chastity and celibacy, but not just yet? Might not the Fabians have prayed (if they had believed in God), 'Make the country socialist, but not just yet'? After all, their position in it, with all its faults and injustices, was comfortable and even delightful, as it would no longer have been if their aim was achieved in their own lifetimes. As to the fact that Fabius was *twice* named dictator, I say no more.

I don't want to give the impression, however, that *Freud à Bloomsbury* is nothing but a tissue of error, far from it.[10] But there is a central irony in the book that the author, still a

---

[10] The author does later call Boswell an historian famous for his style, an odd way of summarising the reasons for his renown.

faithful follower of Freud, fails to see or understand. It suggests that psychoanalysis actually blinds people rather than gives them insight. She describes how the Stracheys attended a psychoanalytical conference in Salzburg, from which Freud, still living in Austria, was absent:

> James and Alix Strachey perceived the palpable unease which reigned at the congress and were astounded by it. 'Psychoanalysis,' wrote James, 'seems to unleash, even analysts, emotional storms from which Freud is not exempt.' For the Strachey couple it was a disappointment to see that not even analysts were wiser or more 'normal' than others…

Considering that psychoanalysis was supposed to be a science rather than a religious sect, one might have thought that such an experience would be disillusioning, but not at all. The eye of faith can not only see what is not there but fail to see the significance of what is.[11]

Or again, take this anecdote about Adrian Stephen, Virginia Woolf's younger brother, who studied medicine and then became a psychoanalyst:

> James [Strachey] regarded him with a friendly irony. "It is said that Adrian at present is in a terrible state and threatens to put a bullet in his head that would be good publicity for Glover [Dr James Glover, Adrian's

---

[11] I have throughout translated the French translation of the English back into English.

psychoanalyst]. If it were in our room, not only would that risk dirtying our carpet, but it would harm our reputation – such that I believe it would be my professional duty to try to stop him. [James Strachey also practised as a psychoanalyst, though he was not a doctor.]

In fact an astonishing number of the early psychoanalysts *did* kill themselves. Whether those inclined to suicide were drawn to psychoanalysis by elective affinity, or whether psychoanalysis itself drove them to it, I do not know. But the author mentions that the famous child analyst, D. W. Winicott, had an analysis lasting ten years. I think I would rather kill myself than have to talk about myself for an hour several times a week for ten years: it would save time.

When the Stracheys published their translation of Freud's case histories, the eminent botanist, Arthur Tansley, himself attracted to the new 'science' and who undertook an analysis with Freud, wrote 'The discoveries of Freud surpass those of Copernicus in astronomy and Einstein in physics... The teachings of Freud are certainly astonishing, and his theories give the impression of being grotesque and bizarre in the extreme – even more than the disgust and general repugnance that they arouse in most people... Freud pushes his investigation much more deeply and painfully than Darwin himself, and is attacked even more strongly...'

This hyperbole, absurd as it is to modern ears, was criticised even at the time. A passage from the book is worth quoting:

The virulent criticisms [of Tansley's article] came with a

well-known refrain: so long as the results of psychoanalysis are not measures, evaluated and proved scientifically, Freud's discoveries represent only gratuitous speculations. A detractor attacked Tansley directly: 'I am convinced that Professor Tansley applies a more rigorously scientific method in his field of botanical science than in this "new psychology": if not, he would not enjoy so good a reputation.

Then the author, Henriette Michaud, asks, 'Who would respond to these *ad hominem* attacks?'

But they are not *ad hominem* attacks, they are making a very serious point about psychoanalysis that has never been properly answered, because it is in the nature of the 'discipline', 'science', 'profession', 'faith', or whatever you call it, to make it impossible to do so.

John Maynard Keynes (according to the book) defended Tansley and psychoanalysis with an intellectual dishonesty or sophistry that is shocking to read:

He [writes the author] put forward the new hypothesis that if Freud had *invented* all the case histories [translated by the Stracheys], whose validity some contested, if none of it had been true, that would be of no importance, for the interest in Freud's examples reside for many in the appeal they have to our own intuitions – and hardly reside in hypothetical inductive verifications or other evaluations.

Keynes went on to say that Freud merited serious attention

because, whether or not his theories please us (or, one might add, whether or not they contain any truth), 'he is one of the most disturbing and original geniuses of this [20th} century.' The same might, of course, have been said of Hitler.

It is known beyond dispute that Freud lied about the outcome of his cases: but if mud sticks, evidence does not. Even Alix Strachey wrote, when two psychoanalysts died at a comparatively early age, 'It seems that God wants to exterminate our detested sect.' Sect was precisely the right word.

In the space of a few pages, the author provides fragments of anecdotes that convey real tragedy. The first concerns Marjory Olivier (a relation of the actor), one of four intellectual sisters who were all Fabians and lived on the edges of the Bloomsbury set.

> Noel Olivier-Richards [Marjory's sister, a doctor], preoccupied for years by her sister's erotomania, asked Karl Abraham to treat her [Abraham was the leading psychoanalyst in Berlin]. But he refused: the case was too serious and Berlin was too far from London. Marjory was interned in a psychiatric hospital for the rest of her life.

Which is to say, for more than forty years. At the beginning of my career, I knew such people. Marjory died in 1974.

The second tragedy, somewhat less grave, concerned Karine, estranged wife of Adrian Stephen, the latter living in the Stracheys' house where, as a practising psychoanalyst, he had his rooms. Despite their estrangement, Stephen's wife and their children:

…came to see him, made noise on the stairs, and shouted (Karine was deaf).

What sorrow is contained in those last three words!

The third tragedy concerns a neighbour of the Stracheys:

> Near James. At 19 Gordon Square, an American called Home Lane set up, giving himself the title of psychoanalyst despite a prohibition by the British Society [of psychoanalysis]. Accused of a sexual assault on a patient in 1924 – just at the time that James Strachey set himself up – he was condemned to deportation as an undesirable alien, and died on the boat taking him back to the United States.

I don't know of what, or whether, Lane was guilty, but even if he were guilty, a lonely and humiliating death on board ship at the age of 50 was likely to have been an excessive punishment.

Of the very few lines of Spanish poetry I have committed to memory, about half are by Antonio Machado. Along with half a million other Spaniards, he fled to France at the approach of Franco's victory. He had his mother with him: he was sixty-four and she eighty-five. There was also his brother José and his sister-in-law Matea, whose three daughters they had sent to Russia, where they did not have a good time, for safety's sake. José later emigrated to Chile where he died in 1958, sorrowful that he had never been able to see his native land again. The three daughters survived Stalinism and rejoined their parents in Chile, though one of them returned to Russia.

Neither Machado nor his mother was in robust health. They spent the night before they arrived in Collioure, just over the French border with Spain, in an abandoned freezing railway carriage. The official welcome they received in France was hardly warmer, but the local people were more generous. The owner of a small haberdashery, Madame Figueros, had put out a table with a thermos of coffee and some bread for the refugees who passed. Exhausted, Machado asked for a seat for his mother and himself. She was confused: she had asked 'Will we arrive in Seville soon?' — a question that gives concrete meaning to the term *second childhood*, for it is the kind of question that children ask from the back of the car. 'Are we nearly *there*, yet?', without quite knowing where *there* is.

Machado asked Madame Figueros to recommend a hotel, and she recommended the Hotel Bougnol-Quintana opposite. There they were warmly welcomed; and it so happened that the stationmaster of Collioure, Jacques Baills, saw Machado's name in the hotel register and, remarkably, recognised the name as that of Spain's greatest living poet. Until then, Machado and his mother had been just two more Spanish refugees. Machado's only baggage was an umbrella, life thus imitating art, for twenty-six years earlier, in his famous poem *En tren* (In Train), he had written:

> For every journey, I
> - always on the wooden bench
> of my third class carriage -

go light of luggage.[12]

Light of luggage: that is the way, metaphorically and perhaps even literally, we should travel through life!

Jacques Baills approached Machado the day after his arrival in the hotel and asked him whether he was *the* Antonio Machado, the great poet. He befriended Machado and brought him books: the stationmaster was a highly cultivated man. He was present at Machado's deathbed only three weeks after he had arrived in Collioure.

Machado's mother died three days later. It is difficult to think of a more tragic or affecting end.

For me, Spanish is the most beautiful language in the world, or at least of those known to me — I would recognise neither Finnish nor Uzbek. The first poem of Machado's that I ever read was *He andado muchos caminos* (I Have Gone Down Many Roads):

> I have gone down many roads.
> I have opened many paths;
> I have sailed a hundred seas,
> and tied up at a hundred shores.
>
> Everywhere I have seen
> caravans of sadness,
> proud and melancholy

---

[12] Yo, para todo viaje
siempre sobre la madera
de mi vagón de tercera –
voy ligera de equipaje.

drunks with dark shadows,

and great know-all pedants
who look, remain silent, and think
they know because they don't drink
the wine of the taverns. [13]

There are bad people who plague the earth, but Machado is
not misanthrope, far from it, for:

… everywhere I have seen
people who dance or play
when they can, and dig
their tiny patch of land.

Never, if they arrive somewhere,
do they ask where they have arrived.
When they travel they ride on the backs

---

[13]   He andado muchos caminos,
he abierto muchas veredas;
he neavgado en cien mares,
y atracado en cien riberas.

En todas partes he visto
caravanas de tristeza,
soberbios y melancólicos
borrachos de sombra negra,

y pedantones al paño
que miren, callen, y piensen
que saben, porque no beben
el vino de las tavernas.

of an old mule,

and they don't know haste,
not even on the days of fiesta.
Where there is wine, they drink wine;
where there is no wine, cold water.[14]

They are good people because modest and unassuming:

They are good people who live,
till the ground, pass by and dream.
and one day like so many
rest under the earth.[15]

---

[14] … en todas partes he visto
gentes que danzan o juegan,
cuando pueden, y laboran
sus cuatros palmos de tierra.

Nunca, si llegan a un sitio,
preguntan adónde llegan.
Cuando caminan, cabalgan
A lomos de mula vieja,

y no cononcen la prisa
ni aun en los días de fiesta.
Donde hay vino, beben vino ;
donde no hay vino, agua fresca

[15] Son buenas gentes que viven,
laboran, pasan y sueñan,
y en un día como tantos
descansan bajo la tierra.

I never think of my own death without thinking of this last verse, veering between the hope that I shall be missed and thus remembered, and the hope that I shall slip away from life as quietly as an uninvited guest from a party, unnoticed and soon forgotten, like the good people of the poem.

Much as I like and even love this poem, the categorical division between good and bad people always worries me because it seems to have the corollary that if only we could get rid of the bad people (assuming that we could identify them correctly, without false positives and false negatives), the world would be a much better place, indeed wholly good. And that is not only false, but exceedingly dangerous.

Machado was much too decent a man to have ever become a dichotomising fanatic. He was a poet, not an ideologue (though he was a firm and unwavering supporter of the Republican side in the Spanish Civil War). One of his poems reminds me very strongly of Housman in its sensibility, its apprehension that time flows in one direction only and that the past is irrecoverable:

> Wayfarer, the way
> Is your footprints, nothing more.
> Wayfarer, there is no way.
> The path is made in walking,
> in walking the path is made.
> On turning to look behind
> you see the path that you
> will never tread again.
> Wayfarer, there is no way

but the wash of the sea.[16]

Compare this with:

> Into my heart an air that kills
> From far young country blows.
> What are those blue remembered hills,
> What spires, what farms, are those?
>
> That is the land of lost content,
> I see it shining plain,
> The happy highways where I went
> And cannot come again.[17]

Is not the melancholy irreversibility of time not also the condition of life having any meaning? Could there be seriousness without it?

For a more, indeed infinitely, painful reflection on the absence of a way, I mention again Gloucester's exclamation, 'I have no way/ And therefore want no eyes.'

---

[16]   Caminante, son tus huellas
el camino, nada mas ;
Caminante, no hay camino,
se hace camino al andar.
Al andar se hace camino,
y al volver la vista atrás
se ve la senda que nunca
se ha de volver a pisar.
Caminante, no hay camino
Sino estaleas en la mar.

[17] A.E. Housman, *A Shropshire Lad*

What use is history (the study of it, I mean, not the mere fact that it exists)? Does it teach us wisdom, in which case is he wisest who knows most history? Does it teach laws by which we may regulate our conduct of affairs well, or by which we may predict the future course of events? Or is the only thing that it teaches the fact that no one ever learns anything from history? Even this implies that there might be lessons to be learned from it, if only people attended to them — which they never do.

Curzio Malaparte's *Technique of the Coup d'État*, published in 1931, suggests not an inevitable historical law, exactly, but a regularity that applies to his time and place, namely Europe in the first half of the twentieth century. His book is in the realpolitik tradition of Machiavelli and also has some similarity with the work of yet another Italian, Antonio Gramsci, who theorised the takeover of the state and society by what might be called the method of termites as opposed to a militarised frontal attack.

Malaparte (who had been born Kurt Erich Suchert, as Italo Svevo had been born Aron Hector Schmitz) was a highly ambiguous figure, an early adherent of Italian Fascism who ended his life in the Italian Communist Party — lukewarmness being evidently not for him. He fell out with Mussolini, was imprisoned and placed under house arrest for several years but was nevertheless appointed a correspondent on the Eastern Front during the Second World War (he had fought in the First). He was a kind of stormy petrel, dangerous adventure for him being the highest form of freedom. I once knew the feeling.

His book on the modern coup d'état reads like a self-help manual for those intent on overthrowing a government, irrespective of the reasons for doing so, though it is also a manual for governments on how to protect themselves from such efforts. Of the morality of overthrow and defence he says nothing. I suppose this is what is meant by the term *political science*: an examination of how things are, have always been and always will be, rather than how they ought to be.

Malaparte starts with an examination of the Russian Revolution, which originally was a coup rather than a revolution in the sense of a mass violent uprising. The revolution followed the achievement of power and was not what gained the power. In Malaparte's version, Trotsky had the major role in the achievement of power, not Lenin: *pace* the latter, Trotsky did not believe in large-scale social forces and mass uprisings as a pre-condition of the overthrow of government (as did the government itself) but in the takeover and occupation of the nerve centres of the state — the telephone exchange, the post office, the stations and so forth — by a comparative handful of trained and determined men acting in well-timed concert. According to the theory, it was not only states in a pre-existing state of decomposition that could be seized by this method but *all* modern states, reliant as they were on the technology of the time. The mistake of governments trying to defend themselves against incipient takeover was that they defended parliament buildings rather than telegraph offices, ministries rather than telephone exchanges. With communications cut, however, parliamentarians and ministers were like puppets whose strings had been cut.

Whether or not the theory is true — whether or not it was true of the October Revolution, whether or not, even if true of that revolution, it would be true of other European countries — one cannot help but wonder what the equivalent technique of disruption and taking control would be in our times. We imagine that our societies are so complex that their governments could not be overthrown by the simple method of Trotsky (as described by Malaparte). Taking control would certainly be much harder than disruption, though the latter might one day be easy, so dependent have we become on the internet. If some evil genius were able to disrupt the internet completely, the lives even of those not addicted to it or who do not use it would soon feel the effects. It is said that supermarkets have three days' supply of food in store: the abundance and vast choice to which we have become so accustomed is, in a sense, an illusion, and (to adapt Marx from a different context) all that is solid melts into the air. Life would soon become a nightmare: no electricity, no fuel, no water, no supplies of anything. When it comes to production and repair, most of us are as helpless as new-born babes. From where, in any large town or city, would the inhabitants obtain water once it ceased to flow from the tap? Oddly enough, E.M. Forster, of all people, foresaw the problem in 1909, the year of my father's birth, in his story, *The Machine Stops*. Mankind in the story has become so dependent on its own technological inventions and upon an overall mechanism whose working no one understands, that when the mechanism breaks down, as all mechanisms eventually do, mankind becomes nothing like a seething mass of maggots in a fisherman's tin of bait.

At any rate, in the event of any severe breakdown it would not take long before people would cry out for the man on the white horse, as Goethe put it, who would restore order at the expense of all freedom. And given that we have come to think that the absence of so many things is an intolerable hardship, the call would come sooner than in previous times.

One of the most interesting chapters of Malaparte's book is that devoted to Hitler, written two years before he came to power: before, in a sense, he was *really* Hitler. The chapter is titled *A Woman: Hitler*. I do not think anyone could use such a title today, for more than one reason: it would simultaneously trivialise the evil of Hitler and be derogatory of women.

In this chapter, Malaparte says that Hitler's fundamental flaw is that he is entirely lacking in masculinity.[18] He is as weak as a chocolate cream, and like many weak people who like to be strong, he mistakes intransigent cruelty for strength. Of course, he needs to surround himself with nonentities because of what would now be called lack of self-esteem. He is envious of the achievements or talents of others and seeks self-elevation by means of the abasement of others. According to Malaparte, this makes him womanly.

Irrespective of the theory's rather dim view of femininity, I am not sure that the term *nonentity* is the one that springs to mind when one thinks of Goebbels, say, or Goering. They were compounded of many vices, but lack of character was not one of them. The problem was precisely their character, not their lack of it. But in a postface, written in 1948, to the

---

[18] I make no reference to the popular song about Hitler's external genitalia.

chapter on Hitler, Malaparte says that he did not have to change a single word of it. Although the chapter mentions Hitler's social programme, neither in the original nor in the postface does he mention his antisemitism.

In a preface to the 1948 edition of the book, however, Malaparte mentions that Mussolini never forgave Malaparte for having thrown him in prison, thus confirming La Rochefoucauld's dictum that we never forgive those whom we have wronged:

> By an order signed by his own hand, he caused an inquiry to be opened to discover whether I was Jewish, in the hope of finding another reason to explain my conduct and justify his. And this in 1936, two years before the racial laws. This singular idea, which remains inexplicable to me, shows just how much his inferiority complex humiliated him.

This raises a question, to which I do not have the answer: when is overconfidence the real thing, and when is it compensation for lack of confidence? And how do you distinguish between the two?

Man, as far as we know, is the only creature that contemplates the possibility of the extinction of its own species, sometimes even with a strange satisfaction.

There is a film of the last thylacine, or Tasmanian tiger, alive before the species became extinct. Of course, the creature in its cage in Hobart Zoo showed no awareness that it was the last of its kind, as presumably the last human alive will, or might. One feels a certain grief on watching this film; I return to it from time to time and think of Gerard Manley Hopkins' poem that begins with the line, 'Margaret, are you grieving over Goldengrove unleaving,' and which ends with 'It is Margaret that you grieve for.' If we as individuals cannot live for ever we have the consolation of the false belief that Mankind is eternal, and therefore that we can add our mite to eternity.

There are, however, those who think the thylacine is not extinct and who devote their lives to proving it. I have both an admiration and a soft spot for them. They have a purpose in life, and unlike many people with a purpose, they are essentially harmless. A negative being difficult to prove, they might even be right, for Tasmania still has much wilderness. There are regular alleged sightings, though none incontrovertible. I suppose they are the secular equivalent of sightings of the Virgin Mary.

As for me, though I am not exactly an explorer of wildernesses, I am fascinated by the thylacine and everything connected with it, from the efforts to resurrect it from samples of its DNA to the psychology of those who mistakenly claim to have seen one from the cab of their pick-up truck. I cannot explain this fascination, or why the extinction of the thylacine should have caught the imagination of so many people. After all, no one goes on a dodo hunt in Mauritius, or searches for a passenger pigeon in North America. Perhaps it is the fact that the top predator of any ecosystem always fascinates us (though that only pushes the question one stage further back, as to why such predators always fascinate us). Perhaps it is the strangeness of the creature itself, though it is surely no stranger than the dodo. Or perhaps it is the fact that the extinction occurred within living memory and the last survivor was filmed, unlike the last survivor of any other species gone extinct — though, incidentally, half the species declared extinct are found again, even a century later. Every time one hears of the finding of a bird or frog or insect supposedly extinct long ago — long ago as mentioned by reference to the duration of human life, that is — one thinks 'And the thylacine?'

In 1898, in the year in which he published *The War of the Worlds*, H.G. Wells published an essay written shortly before titled *The Extinction of Man*. It appeared in a volume titled *Certain Personal Matters*. My copy of this book bears the signatures of two previous owners, separated by nearly a century, the first May 4, 95, and the second 21-11-92, the first of the nineteenth and the second of the twentieth century. Neither marked the century, however: mentally, none other than that in which he was living could have truly existed for the signatory.

In *The War of the Worlds*, mankind faces extinction at the hands (I use the word metaphorically) of the invading Martians and is saved not by its own efforts but by bacteria to which the Martians prove vulnerable, never having encountered them before, and against which they have no defence. Microorganisms in the past could both impede and advance conquest, as for example the penetration of the interior of Africa by Europeans or the Spanish conquest of Mexico and Peru, malaria impeding the first and smallpox advancing the second.

Wells begins his essay on the extinction of Mankind by saying, 'It is part of the excessive egotism of the human animal that the bare idea of its extinction seems incredible to it.' But, as he points out, all previously existing animals that have dominated the surface of the earth have died out and been replaced by creatures very different from themselves. Man's extinction is not incredible, it is inevitable, and it is difficult not to detect a certain glee in Wells as he imagines the kind of beings who will replace it as the dominant creature on Earth. First, he imagines giant crabs (as he imagined them three years earlier in *The Time Machine*), whose pugnacity would be terrifying, though I doubt that Mankind, if it still existed, would not soon develop anti-crab missiles. Then Wells imagines giant cephalopods, octopuses and the like, who might develop land-going potential. Again, these are hardly the stuff of real nightmares, even after a late collation of strong cheese and wine. But then Wells turns more realistic. The ants and other insects might inherit the earth, especially after its surface has been devastated by Man's activities. The current concern about insects is that we are extinguishing too many of them with our pesticide, unbalancing whole ecosystems; but insects are tough and resilient, and some species will emerge triumphant from the agricultural holocaust and see Man off. In the 1970s, I recall, I saw a film (which I loved) which argued that once Man had eliminated himself by means of nuclear war, that then seemed possible and now seems possible again as I write this, insects would inherit the earth.

Wells' last suggestion is that bacteria might do the job (viruses had yet to be discovered). 'There is always the prospect of a new disease,' he writes. 'The bacilli have no more settled down into their final quiescence than have men; like ourselves, they are adapting themselves to new conditions and acquiring new powers... and for all we know even now we may be quite unwittingly evolving some new and more terrible plague – a plague that will not take ten or twenty or thirty per cent, as plagues have done in the past, but the entire hundred.'

In my library, there is a book published almost exactly one hundred years later, titled *Virus X*, by Frank Ryan, that predicts, or at least raises the possibility, of precisely this. Is one terrified or entertained, or both? After all, terror, so long as it remains in the realm of the imagination, has always amused or delighted us.

When V.S. Naipaul called the Ayatollah Khomeini's fatwa against Salman Rushdie 'an extreme form of literary criticism', he demonstrated how British he had become — British of another age, that is, when everyone knew that words were not always to be taken literally.

The British once found murder amusing, at least to read about, for accounts of it were almost always laced with irony. Of course, the closer to murder you got, the more horrible (and usually sordid) it became. This was so obvious that it needed not to be said; and what needed not be said was not said. But those days are now past because people are now so willing or even eager to take offence at words interpreted in their most literal meaning, taking offence being a guarantee for those who need one that their moral sense is still in existence. And moral outrage, besides, is a delightful emotion, one that never lets you down.

I suppose it was Thomas de Quincey who first treated murder with irony, in his famous essay, *On Murder Considered as One of the Fine Arts*, published in 1827. In his essay written 119 years later, *The Decline of the English Murder*, George Orwell lamented ironically that murder in England had become more crude and brutal, less subtle, a tendency which he attributed to the Americanisation of British life and culture. Increasingly, it, murder, failed to have what Sherlock Holmes called its points of interest. Orwell spoke of the golden age of British murder, and I know what he meant. Murder in the golden age was often a matter of poison intruding into a respectable household, or if there were any brutality at all, in a milieu in which such was not to be expected. (Orwell, incidentally, was not the first writer to lament the decline of the English murder: Virginia Woolf's father, Leslie Stephen, did so in an essay in the *Cornhill Magazine* in 1868.) More recently, murder in England has become, it is true, most often a mere matter of loss of self-control in the midst of a fatuous dispute by persons immersed in the mental swamp of modern popular culture, or maybe alcoholic subculture. I was perhaps fortunate that the first murderer whom I ever met was faintly redolent of the golden age, insofar as he was an elderly man (though younger than I am now) with no criminal record, who realised on his retirement just how much he hated his wife, with whom he had never had to spend so much time before.

His crime was deemed to be so extraordinary and unexpected that he was sent to hospital rather than to prison, on the supposition that he must have been either mad or neurologically impaired. At that time, I had never met a murderer before and felt almost honoured to shake the hand that had strangled. I was then a callow young man.

The golden age, to adopt Orwell's periodisation, coincided with ironical writing about murder, and with what would now be considered unacceptable levity. My late friend, the development economist Peter Bauer, used to admire the combination of gaiety and seriousness which the British used to have but have no longer, now mistaking as they do earnestness for seriousness and frivolity for gaiety. At any rate, there was once a time when no one needed to be told, when they read an account of it, that murder is wrong, an infraction of both the legal and the moral code.

I will give a couple of examples of the kind of ironic writing about murder that was once in vogue. I choose them not because they are the best of the genre, but simply because they come easiest to my hand. The first is by Helena Normanton, in her introduction to *The Trial of Norman Thorne: The Crowborough Chicken Farm Murder*. Helena Normanton (1882 – 1957) was the second woman admitted to the English bar and was a campaigner for women's rights. My copy of this book once belonged to Mary, Duchess of Buccleuch, suggesting that the taste for this kind of literature was not confined to the lower, or middle, reaches of society. Here is how Normanton, no reactionary, described the murder:

> On the morning of December 5th, 1924, a young woman named Elsie Cameron was having her hair waved at her hairdresser's. On her return home she attired herself in a new jumper and shortly after midday departed from her parents' house in Kensal Rise for her lover's dwelling near Crowborough. She believed that she was taking her

nuptial journey, and awaited marriage as a result. Before twenty-four hours had passed, the neatly coiffured head had been severed from her shoulders and buried in an old tin in one of the chicken runs on her sweetheart's farm, her dismembered torso having been interred beside it. Such was her journey, such was her fate.

The accused, Norman Thorne, was found guilty and hanged, proclaiming his innocence to the end (an outcome of which Normanton was aware when she wrote the above). The question here is not whether or not Thorne was guilty: it is the irony with which Normanton wrote.[19]

My second example is from a book published in 1950, in the faint afterglow of the golden age, written by a doctor called

---

[19] There is a strong possibility that Thorne was innocent. The chief prosecution medical witness, Sir Bernard Spilsbury, then the pre-eminent forensic pathologist in the country, with such a reputation that the phrase 'Spilsbury called in' made it more or less certain that the accused would hang, or at least be found guilty. But in a book examining some of Spilsbury's famous cases, *Lethal Witness* by Andrew Rose, it is suggested that Spilsbury habitually exaggerated the evidence for the prosecution and underplayed that for the defence, dishonestly making things up as he went along, while simultaneously appearing entirely judicious and disinterested. So it was, Rose alleges, in the case of Norman Thorne. His defence was that Elsie Cameron hanged herself while he was away from his habitation and he then dismembered and buried her when he was in a state of panic. Sir Bernard claimed that there was no post-mortem evidence that Elsie hanged herself, but other pathologists disagreed, probably with reason. In one of his last letters before he was hanged, Thorne said that he was the victim of what he called Spilsburyism: the uncritical acceptance as gospel of all that Sir Bernard said.

Gordon Gwynn, titled *Did Adelaide Bartlett...?* As far as I can tell, Dr Gwynn left no trace in the world, literary or otherwise, or at least not on the internet, other than this book, an examination of the case of Adelaide Bartlett who was accused of having poisoned her husband, Edwin, with the liquid chloroform that was found in his stomach after his unexpected death.

The book begins:

> One New Year's Eve, 1885, Mr Edwin Bartlett returned home from visiting his dentist, and after having taken a meal of oysters, mango-chutney, cake and tea, early next morning was found dead in his bed – a fairly reasonable and deserving sequel.

This is V.S. Naipaul forty years *avant la lettre*. The author goes on to explain the reasons for the universal interest the case aroused at the time:

> ... it was a wife who was accused of killing her husband – an unfailing fascination and the sublimation of uncharitable wishes buried, with varying shallowness, in the subconsciouses of everybody... The Bartlett case exudes a quality that I can only call charm.

Mrs Bartlett, having discovered that her husband was dead, sent her servant, Alice, to fetch the doctor who lived not far away and who was not very pleased to have been woken in the middle of the night.

'Is he really ill?' he asked Alice.

'Yes, sir,' said Alice. 'He's dead, sir.'

I suppose you can't get much more ill than being dead, though I dare say that philosophers might cavil that after death there is no one any longer to be ill. Alice, then, was mistaken: you cannot be both ill and dead.

This exchange between Alice and the doctor reminded me of that between a local man who, in 1949, found a headless body floating in a marsh and called a policemen. When he arrived, the local man said to him, 'There's something not right here.'

'No,' said the policeman, 'there's something not right.'

It is not only English murder that has declined.

Superstition springs eternal in the human mind, and it is probably pointless to cavil at what is eternal. There is a law of the conservation of superstition as there is of energy: and if it does not attach to one thing, it will attach to another.

Le Docteur Vardo would agree with me. Of him, I have been able to discover very little, other than that he published three short books, *Le Charlatanisme et les charlatans en la medicine: Étude psychologique* (Charlatanism and Charlatans in Medicine: A Psychological Study), published in 1867; his doctoral thesis, *De la Misère consideré comme cause des maladies* (Of Poverty Considered as a Cause of Diseases), published in 1843, of which the Bibliothèque nationale de France (the National Library of France) does not possess a copy; and two editions, published in 1851 and 1855 respectively, of his *Précis sur les eaux minérales des Pyrénées* (Short Account of the Mineral Waters of the Pyrenees). Of his character, habits or even professional position I have discovered nothing (admittedly my efforts have been perfunctory). But his book, or booklet — it is only 48 pages long — on charlatanism was published by J.B. Baillière et Fils, the most prominent French medical publisher of the day.

How I came by my copy I can no longer recall: probably I bought it from a bouquiniste on one of the *quais* by the Seine in Paris. It is precisely the kind of unconsidered trifle that I, like Autolycus the Rogue in *The Winter's Tale*, like to snap up. It is the kind of book that booksellers advertise as being *very scarce*, omitting to mention that buyers of it are scarcer still and that they have had it in their stock for years. They put a high price on it and wait for inflation to make it reasonable one day for someone to buy it.

Dr Vardo's preface begins:

> There is an inclination to the marvellous in the human mind itself: it is a need so universal, instinctive and irresistible, that one is forced to admit that it is one of the laws of our being, it is one of the attributes of our nature and, so to speak, one of the conditions of our existence.

It is necessary to take this into account when 'one makes a vain effort to arrest or slow this current, which fatally drags humanity from the laws of reason and good sense, and casts it into the regions of the absurd and the impossible.'

But, asks Dr Vardo, has not the progress of civilisation at least succeeded in enlightening and making more reasonable this taste for the marvellous? He answers with a fine example: 'One must wonder whether the civilised man of our time, who consults turning tables [of the spiritualists, then popular] and who wears medals and amulets to preserve himself against illnesses and other accidents, proves himself to have better sense than the ancients who consulted the flight of birds or than that of the savages who prostrate themselves before their fetishes.'

For Dr Vardo there was a brief period of reason in human history. In the eighteenth century, uniquely in that human history, Mankind stopped 'to contemplate the truth'. But this brief interlude of reason did not last long, and 'it [humanity] soon took again to the route through the centuries and began to travel full sail over the immense sea of foolishness whose depths no sound has ever been able to able to plumb. That is why the idea that the earth revolved around the sun met such obstacles to acceptance while the rotating tables of the spiritualists met with none.'

But what insect is biting him, Dr Vardo imagines his reader asking? Why does he bother those poor charlatans and try to prevent them from deceiving people who want to be deceived? He disclaims all reforming zeal. Peace be to the fools, he says, peace be to the charlatans! He wants to live on good terms with these two halves of humanity, the deceived and the deceivers. He seeks only to describe.

As befits this task, he divides charlatans (in medicine) into two large classes: the public and the private. The former dress in flamboyant costumes and address crowds in the street from the back of carts. They extol absurdly the virtues of some cheaply-produced potion as a panacea. In my study, I have a hand-coloured lithograph of precisely this kind of charlatan, in the style of Daumier but actually by Charles-Émile Jacques

(1813 – 1894),[20] printed and published by Daumier's printer and publisher, which has a charlatan in a rich burgundy velvet coat fringed with gold, haranguing a crowd from the back of an open carriage. Behind him is a man in a vaguely oriental costume looking the other way, as if he cannot bear to listen to this rubbish all over again. Titled *Le Médecin du Roi de Perse* (The King of Persia's Doctor), the text of whose harangue is the following:

> Yes, ladies and gentlemen, there is no illness that can resist my balm… and I left the court of the King of Persia only because everyone had been so radically cured that there was nothing left to do in that country… you can write to that country's authorities and ask them if what I say is not the exact truth!

Vardo's second type of charlatan, who caters to the bourgeoisie and aristocracy rather than to the multitudes, is the private kind. This type of charlatan must appear successful, for example by furnishing his rooms luxuriously. He employs persiflage just as the public charlatan does, but it is of a slightly more subtle nature, polysyllabic and Latinate, because he must impress a more educated but equally gullible public. That the public in general has little judgment in discerning medical merit is suggested to Dr Vardo by the fact that certain members of the medical profession, finding no success despite their merits as legitimate practitioners, adopt

---

[20] He was also a painter of the Barbizon school admired by Baudelaire.

the ways of charlatans, and by doing so attain a success that they never attained before.

It is worth quoting Dr Vardo's conclusion at some length:

> Now, before finishing, let us glance back and, having examined in detail this hideous leprosy of charlatanism that spreads over the face of society, let us wonder whether there is a remedy to oppose it?
>
> The question is hard and embarrassing, and the remedy seems to me more difficult to apply if the ill person cherishes his malady and does not want to be cured. It is obvious, in fact, that there would be no charlatans to deceive the public if the public did not want, at any price, to be deceived, and it is extremely difficult to deprive it of this satisfaction. The charlatan is necessary for its happiness; it would invent him if he did not already exist. There is no human power that would dare, without committing an act of the most odious tyranny, to prevent me from asking advice on my health from the first empiric that I came across, no more than he could be prevented from giving it to me. Apart from fraud, which it is the duty of justice to pursue and punish, we think that rigorous measures would only increase the credit of charlatans and turn them into victims. The human mind is so constituted that is suffices for someone to be persecuted for him to be considered in the right.
>
> Charlatanism answers an imperious need of the masses, which arises from the love of the supernatural; it is from this side that it must be attacked. We have seen that the study of nature, its laws and its phenomena, that the habit

of observation and reasoning, are powerful protection from the seductions of the marvellous; well, it is by rational, logical and philosophical teachings that we shall remedy this evil to a certain extent.

I say to a certain extent because, whatever we do, we shall never succeed in extirpating from the heart of man the original credulity that is a feature of its nature, such that we might consider it a characteristic of the human species and say: Credulity is one of the attributes that distinguishes man from the animals.

Who could gainsay this? Probably no age has had more believers in the healing chakras of the earth than ours; I have just finished reading for review (I should not have dreamed of reading it otherwise) a book by Robert F. Kennedy Jr., son of the assassinated Senator of the United States, in which he repeatedly describes the healing properties of ivermectin and hydroxychloroquine as 'miraculous'.

There was one question that troubled me as I read this little book. Not only had the author written a book about the healing waters of the Pyrenees, belief in which could hardly have been very well founded in science, but this book was written in 1867 when, according to most medical historians, orthodox medicine had almost nothing effective to offer by way of cure and many of its pills, potions and procedures were noxious rather than beneficial. From the point of view of harm-benefit analysis, charlatanism may well have been preferable to Vardo's orthodoxy.

How, then, did it come about that, out of that ineffectual orthodoxy but not out of charlatanism grew that medicine of today without which I, at least, would long since have been dead, and if not dead from one disease, suffering greatly from several complaints that are now well-controlled?

The answer, I think, is to be found in the rear of this little book which contains the publisher's catalogue of his latest books. Though no one would read them now for any other but antiquarian interest, yet one cannot help but be impressed by the seriousness of the more than one hundred and fifty authors, by their evident erudition and their commitment to evidence. Among the names are several still well-known to medical history for their discoveries: Claude Bernard, for example, and Rudolf Virchow. There are some who discovered clinical signs that still bear their names: Trousseau, for example. There are some who first described diseases or syndromes: Bricquet, for example, Duchenne and Falret. Their treatments were powerless, perhaps, but they had a faith, that of Francis Bacon, that knowledge would one day yield power. And for good or evil, they were not mistaken.

If superstition springs eternal, it is at its most dangerous or harmful when it afflicts the intelligent and highly-educated (not necessarily coterminous). It doesn't really matter if someone shudders if a black cat crosses his path, refuses to walk under a ladder, or fears the thirteenth day of the month, especially if it falls on a Friday. The superstitions of the educated and intelligent, however, are more dangerous because the educated and intelligent are the ones who, finally, set the tone of, and even direct, society, insofar as it can be directed; moreover, their superstitions are usually buried under a rubble of rationalisation, and therefore both more difficult to detect and more difficult to oppose. On the foundations of these superstitions may rest an elaborate superstructure supposedly erected for the public good but actually serving private, sectional or individual interests.

Two days after I wrote about the good Dr Vardo, I happened across an interview with Professor Jonathan Zimmerman in a French literary review. The professor holds a chair at the University of Pennsylvania in the history of education. Clearly an intelligent and learned man, he is liberal in the sense of being in favour of unlimited free speech.

The odd thing is, however, that in this interview he shows himself, unwittingly it is true, in favour of precisely the kind of social policies that would tend to inhibit or prevent free speech. In the interview, he rails against (if rails is not too rhetorical a term) the fact that teaching in American universities is wholly an amateur activity, in the sense that the teachers have no formal training in pedagogy and there is no formal assessment of the quality of their teaching. They are, in effect, a law unto themselves; and the result is that no one knows whether teaching in American universities is very good, very bad, or something in between the two, as one old-fashioned physician put it to a patient who had neither cancer nor leukaemia, but multiple myeloma.

The problem (assuming, of course, that it *is* a problem) arose, according to the professor, because American universities were modelled on German ones of the nineteenth century, in which scientists and scholars ruled the roost. Now there is no reason why an eminent or brilliant scholar or scientist should also be a good teacher; perhaps the presumption should be against rather than for this. Teaching, research and scholarship are different, and since universities are teaching institutions, the emphasis should be on good teaching rather than on excellence in research and scholarship. But no effort is made to assess the quality of a teacher's teaching, unlike the effort put into the assessment of the quality of his research. According to the professor, one of the reasons that the effort is not made is that it would be very expensive to make it.

But surely, the interviewer asked him, students in American universities evaluated their teacher? The professor replies, 'Yes, that is what we call the student survey, a questionnaire that the students fill about the course they have taken. It's important, necessary even, but not sufficient.'

What, then, *is* necessary? Again according to the professor, teachers must constantly assess one another, and all PhD candidates should be examined on pedagogy as well as the subject of their research or scholarship. In other words, there should be much more formalisation than there is.

There is not a word in the interview about the possible corruption and demoralisation that might be — would be — brought about by such a system. We already know that one of the reasons for the well-known phenomenon of grade inflation is that teachers are afraid of their students' assessment of them. Assessment of their teachers by their peers would lead to the overgrowth of groupthink and the pursuit of personal vendettas and the suppression of unorthodox thought and approaches, the desire for uniformity now going under the name of *diversity*.

Formal assessment would be a golden opportunity for

bureaucrats to expand their empires, to say nothing of the intellectual corruption that would result. In this connection I remember my first formal assessment as a consultant or senior doctor in the National Health Service. My assessor had a form to fill in with obligatory questions to ask me. One of them was 'Have you any concerns about your probity?'

I said to my assessor that I would answer this question if he would first answer two of mine. He asked me what they were.

'The first is, What kind of person would answer such a question?'

'And the second?'

'What kind of person would ask it?'

'Oh,' he said, 'I know all that. But we just have to get through this as quickly as possible.'

A single brilliantly-framed question (that is to say, brilliantly-framed if it was with conscious intention) destroyed the probity of two persons at once, who asked and answered a question that they knew was fatuous or worse, merely that they could continue in their present positions, thereby turning them into careerists and placeholders.

This is not to deny, of course, that there are lazy, incompetent or even mad university teachers. It is in the nature of large human groups that all types are to be found within it. My experience of my teachers, however (and for what it is worth), is that they were far better teachers than I was a student. Without any compulsion except an inner drive to do their best, most of them did far more than they could have been obliged to do, which is more than could have been said of me.

The professor's mind (in my opinion, which may be

mistaken) is in the grip of a peculiar modern superstition, that for every human problem, such as deficient teaching in universities, there is an equal and opposite form to fill in, or other procedure to be followed, that will solve the problem and restore the earth to its natural state of perfection. The professor lives in a world in which procedures have no effects other than the ones ostensibly aimed at. He comes across, however, as a very amiable man.

As I flicked through *Make Light of It*, William Carlos Williams' collected short stories, I saw, or thought I saw, a story titled *Against Gentility*. Ah, gentility: who will speak up for it these days (though the date of publication of the book, 1950, hardly counts as *these days*)? Gentility, the word, has the ring of the petty bourgeois about it, the outdated pseudo-refinement of antimacassars, patchouli, aspidistra and crooked fingers as teacups are raised to the lips, of hypocrisy and snobbery.

In the year 2000, I happened to read an obituary of Ian Dury, a punk musician who was partially paralysed in childhood by polio. I don't know why I read it: normally I would not have done so, but Dury was in some ways an admirable man, brave and determined, and with a good sense of humour. The song that propelled him to fame was *Hit Me with Your Rhythm Stick*, which had amusing and intelligent lyrics:

> In the deserts of Sudan
> And the gardens of Japan
> From Milan to Yucatan

Every woman, every man

Hit me with your rhythm stick
Hit me, hit me.
Je t'adore, ich liebe dich...

In the wilds of Borneo
And the vineyards of Bordeaux
Eskimo, Arapaho,
Move their body to and fro

Hit me with your rhythm stick
Hit me, hit me
Das ist gut! C'est fantastique...

Only someone talented, amusing and with a fund of education could have written this.

One sentence in the obituary struck me very forcibly. Dury, it said, had rebelled against what he thought was the false gentility of his school and had adopted the accent of South London in the way he spoke.[21] I thought this rather odd and, in a way, highly significant, for here was an adolescent adopting a speech that was not his own *in the name of authenticity*. At one time, ambitious young persons would have a mode of speech more genteel than their own, not in the name of authenticity but of social advance. Dury's decision, by

---

[21] When you look at pictures of English rock musicians as young children, you are often struck by their innocent-looking respectability. In another age, you can't help thinking, they would have grown up to be churchwardens, bank managers, etc.

contrast, was an example of what might be called romantic proletarianism, the proletariat being seen as somehow more genuinely human, more sincere, less artificial, more natural, than any other stratum of society — real in a way that other strata are not. Indeed, the lower the scale you go, the more authentic you become — in the sense that human excrement is more real than human thought.

In fact, I had misread the title of Williams' story: it was *Ancient Gentility*, not *Against Gentility*. The author was not against gentility at all, at least not in this story. He was, of course, a doctor and paediatrician as well as a poet, the only other paediatrician-poet known to me being Robert Bridges, the only doctor to have been Poet Laureate, and whose book-length poem, *The Testament of Beauty*, now adorns the shelves of every second-hand bookshop, unsold for many years: when once I bought a copy, you could have felled the bookseller with a feather.

Both Bridges and Williams practised at a time when childhood diseases were frequently fatal and real remedies practically non-existent. Neither had to plumb the depths: the depths came to them.

Williams' *Ancient Gentility* is very short, a mere three pages. It recounts a house-call a doctor pays to an old Sicilian immigrant and his wife in New Jersey. They speak no English and are too poor to pay him anything, but as he leaves the house the old man hands him a small silver box. He does not know what to do with it and at first thinks it might be in lieu of payment. But no: it is a snuffbox, and the old man wants to share his snuff with the doctor. Such is the ancient gentility of the title.

This put me in mind of two episodes in my own career. The first was in rural Shropshire where I was acting as a locum general practitioner. I remember the weather and the landscape as having been glorious: certainly, the latter a true memory. In those days, it was part of the practice's routine to visit old ladies living on their own to check that they were all right. For them, the doctor's visit was an event: they had tea and cake laid out. A medical patina was given to the visit by the taking of their blood pressure. It all seemed very civilised, but I am sure that this would now be frowned upon as inefficient. Besides, there are now too many old ladies living on their own for it to be feasible.

One day I received a call from a man in his mid-eighties. He was living on his own in a cottage in a certain squalor common in bachelorhood, and he was now too weak to get out of bed. I visited and found him not far short of moribund. He was grossly anaemic, and he told me that he had been bleeding from his rectum for several months. He had also lost a lot of weight. At his age, this was likely to signify only one thing.

'Why didn't you call me before?' I asked.

'I didn't like to call you because I know you're busy, doctor,' he replied.

As a very young man, I was taken aback by this, by its illogicality. What could a doctor have been busy with that was more important than this man's case? Then I was struck by the nobility of his answer. Here was a man who, even in severe distress, thought of others as being more important than himself. There was something fine in his self-effacement, a world away from that of selfies.

The second case was in Africa. Someone whom I had treated there brought an old man (old as I then thought him to have been, not as I now would consider him to be) who was very short of breath. Examination soon showed that he was in heart failure, and I gave him such treatment as I could. From a purely bureaucratic or administrative point of view, he was not entitled to be treated by me, but I disregarded this small matter.

A few days later, the old man returned bearing a small basket. In it, covered with straw, were five eggs, his means of thanking me. In that time and place, this was a real sacrifice on his part, a precious gift to have given me — perhaps the most precious that I have ever received.

Anyone who has long worked in a prison, as I have, must wonder how he himself would react to imprisonment. He may even, especially if he eats cheese late at night, suffer dreams or nightmares of being so imprisoned. Former policemen are not well-liked by fellow-prisoners, to say the least of it, and though in my fifteen-year career as a prison doctor I never saw a former prison officer or employee of a prison himself imprisoned, I should imagine that such a one would have a very hard time indeed. I can console myself that if I were now imprisoned, my career has been so long over that no prisoner would now recognise me from my former life: though it must be added that prisoners have a kind of bush telegraph that acts as swiftly and possibly more accurately than the social media.

From time to time there would be received into the large prison in which I worked a prisoner of an unexpected social type — a cardiologist, say, or a university professor. When this happened, I was anxious lest he should be suicidal, for I supposed that imprisonment would be especially hard to bear for him. I recalled that when I was about ten, I had a friend who appeared to have no father, which in those days was most unusual. Then one day the father turned up, a man I suppose in his late thirties or early forties, who was wearing smoked glasses — again, unusual in those days. He had just been released from prison, most probably having served his time for fraud, and never shall I forget his furtive, haunted look, that of a man who could scarcely face the world. He exuded a kind of indelible shame which must have meant that, at heart, he was a respectable man, not the type of young man who regarded a term of imprisonment in the light of a campaign medal.

To my surprise, however, the highly educated prisoner adapted quickly and well to imprisonment, at least soon after the initial shock, and I wondered why this was.

The answer is found in Dostoyevsky's episodic semi-autobiographical novel, *The House of the Dead*, in which Dostoyevsky uses the old literary conceit of having come across the unpublished memoirs of his protagonist — namely himself.

He, Alexander Petrovich Gorianchikov, is an educated man, a political prisoner (as was Dostoyevsky himself, of course) rather than a common criminal. He is saved, as it were, by his determination to observe everything around him in his unaccustomed, albeit atrocious, surroundings, in the way of a naturalist. Included in this is observation of himself: and it is his ability to distance himself from his direct and immediate experience that allows him to derive something useful from it, however horrible or unwanted it may have been. The ability to double one's consciousness, to become a disinterested observer of, as well as participant in, his own experience is vital to retaining some equanimity in adversity, and this ability of educated people explained why they fared better than I had expected.

Of course, I don't want to minimise the adversity of that adversity. And often I wondered what would be the worst aspect or aspects of imprisonment, and I found it in Dostoyevsky:

> How terrible it would be never for a single minute to be alone for the ten years of my imprisonment! At work to be always with a guard, at home with two hundred fellow prisoners!

The combination of enforced social promiscuity and loneliness (because in prison there are no real friendships) would be to me truly terrible. In the prison in which I worked a man who had behaved badly was placed temporarily in an isolation cell, there to await what was called *adjudication* by a senior official who would mete out to him some punishment or another (if he were not acquitted), usually a loss of privileges for a certain time. Among my strange duties was that to ensure that any prisoner in an isolation cell was not suicidal or otherwise suffering unduly, or mad; and on my visits, I could not help but think that an isolation cell was the only accommodation in the prison that would be tolerable to me. It was silent 'down the block', as it was called, whereas everywhere else in the prison a permanent cacophony reigned. Many of the prisoners were habituated to the noise and indeed came from social backgrounds in which silence was so unusual that it would have caused them anxiety; but I am almost as morbidly sensitive to noise as Roderick Usher or Marcel Proust, such that the perpetual noise of prison would be to me the worst of tortures.

There are many things about prison life that have not changed fundamentally since Dostoyevsky's time, which would no doubt be taken by many as *per se* an indictment of prison as an institution. There are many passages in *The House of the Dead* that put me in mind of what I myself had seen and heard.[22] The prisoners in the book gang together to complain about the quality of the food they received, which they never did about the cruelty of the corporal punishment to which they were subjected; and I remember a senior prison officer telling me that the most important thing in keeping order in prison (which could only be done with the cooperation of the prisoners) was the quality of the food. Get that wrong, and the prison became ungovernable.

The account of the attempted escape from *The House of the Dead* took me back to the only successful escape during my time at the prison. A prisoner took an overdose with the express intention of being removed to outside hospital. He was guarded by two officers who sat at his bedside while he appeared to be sleeping as a consequence of the overdose that he had taken. There was a television in the ward and relayed

---

[22] Apparently, *From the Dead House* would be a better, or at any rate more accurate, translation of Dostoyevsky's title, but I use the more familiar title.

a cricket match in which the officers were interested. While they were watching it, the prisoner suddenly woke, stood up and dived headfirst through the window above his bed, the ward being on the ground floor. He got clean away but was recaptured very soon after because he went straight home to his mother. This kind of thoughtless impulsiveness would not have surprised Dostoyevsky; in fact, he would have predicted it.

Naturally, when I started to work in the prison, my first question was Dostoyevsky's: 'How should I behave, what attitude should I take up towards these people?' At first, I wanted to be liked, to accede to every request of the prisoners: for, as I told myself, there but for the grace of God go I, and when you are locked up, surely any sign of consideration or kindness must come as a cup of water in the wilderness? But I soon came to realise that this would be interpreted, in that brutal world, as mere weakness rather as than friendship offered to the friendless, and I soon came to Alexander Petrovich's view (he was of high social class compared with most of the prisoners):

> I made up my mind to behave as simply and independently as possible, not to make any special effort to get on intimate terms with them, but not to repel them if they desired to be friendly themselves; not to be afraid of their menaces and hatred, and as far as possible to affect not to notice… in fact, not to seek to be regarded as a comrade by them. I guessed that they would be the first to despise me if I did.

In short, I realised that it was more important to be respected than liked, for in prison another horrible aspect of the life is that a desire to be liked is an invitation to exploitation, other relations being purely instrumental in nature. Being respected, by contrast, cut through or avoided an immense amount of useless trouble.

Some things have changed since Dostoyevsky's time, however. He tells us that spies and informers were tolerated in his prison camp. In my time, no form of prison life was lower than an informer, unless it were a child-molester. On the other hand, as in Dostoyevsky's day, prisoners had a fondness for animals. It was relations with humans that they found so difficult; and animals offered them a chance to love and be loved in return, when so many of them were drawn from a loveless world.

In the year of my birth (1949) a book of astonishing erudition was ready for the press, but a little erratum slip inside said that, contrary to the date given on the title page, and owing to post-war production difficulties, the book would not go on sale till 1950. It was Eric Partridge's *A Dictionary of the Underworld British and American: Being the Vocabularies of Crooks, Criminals, Racketeers, Beggars and Tramps, Convicts, the Commercial Underworld, the Drug Traffic, the White Slave Traffic, Spivs*. It was 806 pages long and contained, according to a swift calculation made from a few recto and verso pages taken at random, about 20,000 entries, many with detailed etymologies indicating intimate acquaintance with an arcane literature with such titles as *Hooligan Nights* and *The Mark of the Broad Arrow*.

In his foreword, Partridge says that cant, in the sense of the language of the underworld, is remarkably conservative: the irony of this remark being that the word *cant* is now rarely if ever used in this sense. Partridge makes it in the context of apologising or excusing himself for the fact that his book, thanks to certain little local difficulties such as the Second World War, was not completely up to date. Real scholars such as he, I imagine, are apt to consider world events as but hindrance to the progress of their scholarship: though it is only fair to point out that Partridge, a New Zealander by origin, was wounded in the First World War. He spent the subsequent fifty years in the reading room of the British Museum.

If cant, in his sense, is mainly conservative, it must be that it becomes more impoverished than enriched over time, because the great majority of entries in the dictionary are no longer current, at least to my, admittedly limited, knowledge. To take one significant example: *Reading one's sheet.* This means 'to examine one's clothes (not only one's shirt) for lice. According to Partridge, it had been used by tramps since 1910 and was, at the time of publication, still 'extant'. He says that it was first used in the British military.

Two things are worth observing here, first of which is the decline of live infestation among the poorest in our society, the second being the disappearance of tramps from our roads, fields, haystacks and barns. A true tramp is no more to be found than is a cooper or a carter or a wheelwright. When I was a boy, there were still, just about, tramps in the sense of gentlemen of the road, those who actually chose a wandering life, rather than what we have now, the schizophrenic or drug-addicted homeless, whose journeys are short, from shop entrance to shop entrance. Tramps were conscious and philosophic rejecters of a more settled and prosperous way of life: they were true lovers of freedom and accepted its consequences. No one could now write a book such as W.H. Davies' *The Autobiography of a Super-Tramp*.

As for the decline of lice, I cannot help but see it as a sign of progress, and I would not lament if they went extinct. Luckily, I have never been parasitised by them, but I have been parasitised by two kinds of insect, the tumbu fly and a jigger, both in Africa, and I have twice been parasitised by ticks or mites, having once caught scabies from a patient with the Norwegian type, and once having caught, or been caught by, a tick while sleeping on my grass in France. I recommend a life free from such ectoparasites.

When I turn at random to pages in the dictionary containing various expressions that begin with the verb 'hit', I find many that I have never heard before, such as 'hit the gong' for smoking opium (perhaps because no one smokes opium any more, there being so many worse alternatives). 'Hit the pipe' is another expression for the same thing, similarly redundant. To 'hit the pots' is to drink to excess, a term used in George C. Henderson's book of 1924, *Keys to Crookdom*. My favourite expression for such drinking that I heard from a patient was 'The beer went mad', but I think that this was a purely personal invention rather than an expression in wide use.

'Hit the hay,' according to Partridge, meant to smoke marijuana, as well as the more familiar (and still current in my early years, a spill-over from tramps' argot) going to bed. The most common expression used by prison officers in my time for cannabis, incidentally, was 'wacky baccy', because it was so often the cause of a transient psychotic state or bizarre behaviour. A man in prison who, having been normal, suddenly went mad was assumed to have smoked cannabis, or taken some other drug, a clinical judgment since it was rarely possible to confirm the diagnosis toxicologically. Interestingly, *speed*, meaning amphetamines or their analogues, does not appear in Partridge.

It is seventeen years since I was employed in prison, and no doubt there are now expressions that I have not heard, just as there were several that were in common use in my time that do not appear in Partridge's vast compendium. I was surprised to discover, for example, that the term *nonce*, for sex-offender, was not included, and so must first have been used after 1949, for I do not think that Partridge would have missed a term in such wide circulation as it was when I worked in prison had it then existed. (Perhaps later editions of the dictionary include it, which would provide a clue as to the date of its first appearance, if not to its etymology, which is still a matter of dispute.) Expressions such as *on the in* and *on the out*, for being in or out of prison, that suggest subliminally that imprisonment is part of normal life, are not in Partridge, though very common parlance among prisoners in my day. For example, a prisoner often said to me 'There's nothing for me on the out' to explain why he committed an act that was certain to land him back in prison: a sad commentary on the life he led, or expected to lead, as a free man.

When I look through Partridge, I think back to my own fifteen years of prison life, albeit not as a prisoner or *con*, as the prison officers called their wards (a term found in Partridge), or *body* as the officers called a prisoner when they brought one to see me in my clinic. 'Shall I bring the bodies up, sir?' an officer would ask me when I arrived in the clinic. *Body* in this sense is not found in Partridge. Another expression not found there, and which has since gone out of use though it was still just about current when I started, is *the black aspirin*, for the prison officer's boot. To 'give a prisoner the black aspirin' was to kick him. It went out of use for one of two reasons, or perhaps for both: first, there was a decrease in the impunity with which officers could abuse prisoners, and second because boots ceased to be part of their uniform.

The prisoners, of course, had other expressions not to be found in Partridge. Many of them concerned drug-taking and addiction, much more prevalent than in Partridge's time. Crack, of course, did not then exist as a substance, but *cold turkey* appears in the dictionary as 'a form of "cure"', the addict being taken off his drug at once and being given various body-building tonics to restore his health', though interestingly this is not the first meaning given to the phrase, that being 'French leave: a deportation without explanation'. (A *cold-turkey rap* was 'an accusation, a charge, against a person caught in the act'.) There is no mention of the goose-flesh that is a physical sign of withdrawal from heroin or the like, but in my time a third bird was often invoked to describe withdrawal, as in 'I'm clucking' or 'I'm doing my cluck', chicken being more familiar to them than goose or even turkey flesh. 'Don't you mean gobble rather than cluck?' a prison doctor acquaintance of mine used to ask.

Some of the expressions used by the prisoners delighted me.

Prisoners who feared that I might send them to psychiatric hospital, where they thought, or had heard rumours, that conditions were worse than in prison, would ask anxiously 'You're not going to nut me off, are you, doctor?' And prisoners returning from court where they had been sentenced to life imprisonment would say, not necessarily with bitterness or disappointment, 'The judge lifed me off', as if he had taken the decision as lightly as brushing off a fly.

Perhaps the most extraordinary expression that I heard, and in in which I took a guilty delight, was one that described the denouement of a dispute between criminals, namely 'He was shown the red card.' This is an expression taken, of course, from football, when the referee holds up a red card to send a player off the field because of an egregious foul he has committed. A criminal who has been shown the red card has been killed by his rival, shuffled off this mortal coil, the football field of life.

I return to the figure of Dr Vardo, not because he is remembered in history, but because he is forgotten by it, as most of us inevitably will be. I noticed on the internet a copy for sale of his thesis published in 1843, *De la misère consideré comme cause de maladies*, and sent off for it straight away, thinking that, as a charitable act, I would leave it to the *Bibliothèque Nationale de France* which, as I have mentioned, does not possess a copy. Of course, I will probably never get round to it.

Dr Vardo's thesis was defended in public on 30th August, 1843, and has a dedication that implies that he had been an orphan early in life:

To my uncles and aunt Beneyteau. You took the place of mother and father to me: receive, therefore, the homage of my first effort. It is very little in return for so many sacrifices; but believe at least that I will always preserve filial feelings for you.

It is dedicated also to his brother and sister:

You were always my best friends, I will never cease to be your devoted brother.

Having been for some time a ship's surgeon, Dr Vardo includes a lieutenant in France's Royal Navy (it was during the reign of Louis Philippe, the Citizen-King), M. Philippe Lescure, chevalier de la Légion d'honneur, in his dedication: Testimony to my esteem and friendship.

And finally, he dedicates this opuscule of 52 pages — the fruit nevertheless of what was probably an immense labour — to his friend and fellow countryman [meaning of the same region of France] Compeyrot, 'Testimony to the most sincere attachment and the liveliest sympathy.'

I don't know how sincerity jumps off a page, or by what rational means one could measure it, but it seems to me that in this case it does so jump.

Dr Vardo was evidently a ship's surgeon for some time, for he introduces the subject of his thesis thus:

Used to living for several years among men for whom prolonged tiredness, a crude and sometimes unhealthy diet, and bad weather and living conditions were the cause of most of their diseases, I was naturally obliged to apply myself to studying the influence of these causes and the nature of the diseases that they caused. In addition, I purposed to deal in my thesis with the hygiene of sailors. But on studying this subject on a wider scale, I realised that the [question of] this hygiene did not belong to sailors alone, but that it was common almost exactly to the most numerous class of society, that it was that of workers, of the indigent, and of all those who, far from enjoying the comforts, often lack the necessities of life that they are forced to buy at the price of hard and even fatal labour.

The connection between ill health and poverty was so obvious that Dr Vardo did not think that statistics were necessary to prove it, but those few that he did provide were telling (of course, statistics were far fewer and less sophisticated in his time and the statistical mode of thinking, that seems now almost second nature to us, far less established). Vardo cites the work of Louis René Villermé, one of the pioneers of what was to become almost the queen of the medical sciences, epidemiology:

The statistical researches of M. Villermé demonstrate that among those aged 20 to 21 years old, those who belong to the poor class are less fit by their size, their constitution, and their health for military service. In order to find a hundred men in fit condition to bear arms, it requires 193 conscripts among the comfortable classes and up to 342 among the poor classes.

The fact that even half the young rich of the time were deemed unfit is surely testimony to the state of health of the population as a whole, all the more so as the standard of fitness required was probably not very high.

Among ordinary infantrymen in the army, the mortality was 2.23 per cent per annum, while it was 1.08 per cent per annum among sub-officers, who were merely somewhat better off than infantrymen.

Dr Vardo quotes some contemporary English statistics — and England, as Dr Vardo says, was somewhat in advance at the time of France in the matter of health protection of workers:

> Of 1078 children who had worked in textile factories, only 22 reached the age of 40 and 9 the age of 50. Of 824 workers, the majority young, there were only 183 who enjoyed good health! 240 were in delicate health, 258 were ill, 43 were stunted, 100 suffered from swelling of the ankles and knees, and 37 were rachitic.

Dr Vardo says, surely with reason, that this is unanswerable. The concept of progress is not very fashionable among those for whom grievance is the highest state of the human mind, but a few pages of Dr Vardo are sufficient to show just how much progress, for whatever reason, we have made.

Dr Vardo also argues statistically that madness is caused by poverty. Among the rich, only half of madmen had mad parents, while among the poor, only a third had. He rejects the argument that the difference is caused by the intermarriage of the rich, because the poor, he says, also intermarry. It is the condition of the poor that drives them mad.

The doctor cannot cure poverty, says Dr Vardo, but he can advise how to obviate or prevent some of its worst effects. And there is one product that can alleviate some of the woes of the poor: tobacco.

I write this on the hundredth anniversary to the day (May 31, 1922) of the execution by hanging at Gloucester Gaol of Major Herbert Rowse Armstrong for a murder that he may not have committed and for which he should not in any case have been convicted (even if guilty). He maintained his innocence to the end, but guilty men have done the same, so that such a protestation is no evidence one way or the other: but the hangman, John Ellis, claimed that his last words were, 'I'm coming, Kate!', Kate having been the wife whom he was alleged to have poisoned with arsenic more than a year earlier. If Ellis was speaking the truth, surely Armstrong's last words pointed to his innocence, for Kate would hardly have welcomed him to the *au-delà* if she thought that he had been her poisoner down below. But Ellis might have been sensationalising.

On the eve of his execution, Armstrong wrote a dignified and moving letter to his solicitor, T.A. Matthews (on prison paper whose design remained identical for at least ninety years afterwards), the evening before his execution:

My dear Matthews,

My heart was too full today to say

all I wished [Matthews had just visited him]. Thank you, my friend, for all you have done for me. No one could have done more. Please convey also to all your staff my gratitude for the ungrudging work they put in. No team could have worked more loyally or with more devotion to duty.

Ever your faithful friend,
H. Rowse Armstrong

Under sentence of death, then, Armstrong was very dignified. He also thanked the warders for their kindness to him and maintained his courteous manner to the end. When the governor of the prison said to him that he didn't like this hanging business, Armstrong replied, with what degree of irony history does not record, 'Yes, I am sure it must be most unpleasant for you.' In his book on hanging — against hanging, that is — Arthur Koestler says that the English don't seem to object to hanging, in fact they seem quite to like it.

Ellis claimed that he was told to be gentle with Armstrong (the only solicitor ever to have been executed in England) because he was a prisoner of a usual type from usual: for he was told, 'You won't have sent away a man like him in all your twenty-one years' experience, he's not of the ordinary type.' Eighty years after, prison officers would sometimes bring a prisoner for a consultation with me with the words, 'He's not your typical con, sir,' meaning that he was well-educated or well-spoken, or refined, well-mannered and of relatively gentle birth.

How would I have behaved before execution for a crime of which I knew myself to be innocent? In my young days, I suspect, I would have raged, raged against the killing of the light, but for the last twenty years or so (I think) I would have accepted my fate with a shrug, as a thing of no importance, more concerned, like Armstrong, with conserving my dignity than with anything else. At least, I hope so.

Armstrong did not receive a fair trial. The judge, Charles Darling, was outrageously biased against him, accentuating the case for the prosecution in his charge to the jury and omitting the strong case for the defence. The other villain of the piece was again the famous pathologist, Sir Bernard Spilsbury, who insinuated a lie by claiming that he had not only dealt with many cases of arsenic poisoning but had done research on it (he had not). His evidence was scientifically flawed, to Armstrong's great detriment, and three questions arise. Could he have known that his evidence was mistaken? If he could have known, did he in fact know it? If he did know it, did he testify in the way he did nevertheless because he was convinced *a priori* that Armstrong was guilty? To these questions, a definite answer can be given to the first two. He could have known that what he was saying was wrong, and he implicitly admitted under cross-examination that it might be wrong, while still maintaining his original position that Armstrong's wife had been poisoned and Armstrong was the only possible poisoner. It is difficult to avoid the conclusion that both Darling and Spilsbury were determined to see Armstrong hanged, though why they should have taken so strongly against him is a mystery.

Three young children, their mother already dead, were orphaned by Armstrong's execution, and one averts one's mind from contemplating the consequences for them.

At least five and a half books have been written about the case (the half being also devoted to the case of another solicitor, Harold Greenwood, accused of having poisoned his wife with arsenic, who was acquitted shortly before Armstrong was tried, not very far from where Armstrong was tried). Three of the five full books cast doubt on the verdict without positively asserting his innocence, while two maintain his guilt. The Armstrong case is also the subject of innumerable chapters in books.

Hay-on-Wye, known until 1948 just as Hay, where Armstrong practised as a solicitor, is a little town well known to me that sits astride the Welsh border. It is one of two small towns whose best-known resident was a poisoner, or an alleged poisoner executed for his crime or crimes, the other being Rugeley in Staffordshire, home of the man once known as the Prince of Poisoners, Dr William Palmer. The pubs in Rugeley still have — or at least had, when I visited them — what might be called *Palmeriana* on their walls, nothing of consequence having happened in Rugeley since 1856, when he was hanged at Stafford Gaol before a public said to number 30,000. As he approached the hastily erected scaffold, he turned to the hangman and asked, 'Is it safe?'

Long after Armstrong was executed, Hay became famous as the first town in the world to be almost entirely devoted to the sale of second-hand books. I went there nearly fifty years ago with some friends. It was a fine day, but there were very dark and menacing clouds on the horizon as we approached the town. I said, 'Let's make Hay while the sun shines,' a pun of which I was inordinately proud.

If being memorialised in a number of books counts as

success in life, Herbert Rowse Armstrong was a success. The latest book, published to coincide with the centenary of his death, is titled *The Poisonous Solicitor: The True Story of a 1920s Murder Mystery*, by Stephen Bates. It seems to me excellent and fair-minded, and it told me things about the case I did not know, though I had read the other four and a half books about it. I have two little extraneous quibbles about it, however. The first is the use of the pusillanimous term *sex-worker* for prostitute, while alluding unfavourably to the hypocritical straight-lacedness of the society in which Armstrong lived. But surely this euphemism is just as dishonest as the straight-lacedness complained of? Is a pimp now to be called a *sex work facilitator*, or some such?

My second quibble is about a sentence in which Hay in the 1920s is described as being lamentably backward:

> It is to be doubted that Modernism, the arts movement of Picasso and Matisse, of Le Corbusier and Ezra Pound, had reached the [Wye] Valley except perhaps to be laughed at in philistine magazines such as *Punch*.

Whatever one thinks of Picasso, Matisse or Ezra Pound (Matisse by far the greatest of them), Le Corbusier was in a different category. His fascist architecture and urbanism (he was a fascist not metaphorically but literally, and in my view it shows in his designs) ruins every townscape or cityscape in which it appears. He was a monster of egotism, and his talent was in the fields of self-promotion and intellectual thuggery rather than in architecture. To read him — he wrote more than he built — is to despise him. He was incapable of logical or consecutive thought or expression and issued only ex cathedra diktats. Among his notable schemes was that to expel millions of Parisians from Paris under the Occupation because he thought they had no business to be there in the first place. Le Corbusier never said — or glimpsed, his eyesight was notoriously bad — a city that he did not wish to destroy with concrete towers. Technically, he was a gross incompetent — his flat roofs in rainy climates leaked, which you would hardly have to have been an architect to predict — and his enormous success, as measured by his influence worldwide, some deep-seated cultural pathology, whose cause I confess that I have not fully diagnosed, but which I suspect was connected to the cataclysm of the First World War.

One of the delights of driving to Hay-on-Wye from my home is that there is not a building *en route* that has been influenced by Le Corbusier, and it comes as a profound relief, like the peace and calm after a crisis in a case of pneumonia, which I have experienced.

'If we wish to know the force of human genius,' wrote Hazlitt, 'we should read Shakespeare. If we wish to see the insignificance of human learning, we may study his commentators.'

Something is not right just because someone famous said it, of course, but I know what Hazlitt meant. Even one of Shakespeare's greatest commentators, Doctor Johnson, said something similar in his introduction to his edition of Shakespeare's works. 'It is not very grateful [gratifying] to consider how little the succession of editors has added to this author's power of pleasing,' he wrote.

Doctor Johnson remarks that in the works of the various editors of Shakespeare, 'the various readings of copies and different interpretations of a passage, seem to be questions that might exercise the wit, without engaging the passions.' But no: arguments about Shakespeare and his work are acrimonious. 'Whether it be that such *small things make men proud*, and vanity catches small occasions; or that all contrariety of opinion, even in those that can defend it no longer, makes proud men angry; there is often found in commentaries a spontaneous strain of invective and contempt, more eager and venomous than is vented by the most furious controversialist in public against those whom he has been hired to defame.'

The authorship question — that of who *really* wrote Shakespeare — did not exist in Doctor Johnson's time, but the reader of the last passage will recognise at once the acrimony with which it is carried on and the utter contempt in which the advocates of Bacon, Oxford, Marlowe, Rutland, etc.,[23] hold in particular those whom they call with derision the *Stratfordians*, that is to say the benighted or deluded souls who persist in believing that Shakespeare the author was Shakespeare the young man from Stratford.

I love the authorship question precisely because there is so little at stake: and, as Dr Kissinger once remarked, the reason that academic quarrels are so bitter is that there is so little at

---

[23] More than sixty candidate authors have been put forward.

stake.[24]

It is always worth reading Doctor Johnson for his robust common sense and for his ability to say things that are both obvious and that come as a revelation. For example, he describes a problem that I have often faced in a slightly different context, and which many others must have faced:

> I found many passages [in Shakespeare] which appeared to me likely to obstruct the greater number of readers [i.e. the majority], and thought it my duty to facilitate their passage. It is impossible for an expositor to write too little for some, and too much for others.

As a commentator on social or medical affairs, I have often been caught between the Scylla of anecdote and the Charybdis of statistics. If I write an anecdote, I am accused of anecdotalism, with the implication of dishonest selectivity in making my point; if I use statistics, I am accused of dryness and lack of concreteness or truth to life. There is, as Doctor Johnson found, no perfect balance to suit all tastes.

Doctor Johnson animadverted on the edition of a previous editor of Shakespeare, William Warburton:

> The original and predominant error of his commentary is acquiescence in his first thoughts; that precipitation which is produced by consciousness of quick discernment; and that confidence which presumes to do,

---

[24] As with much of what Dr Kissinger said, this is more plausible than true. What goes on in the academy is ultimately of great importance for a modern society, for good or ill.

by surveying the surface, what labour only can perform,
by penetrating the bottom.

I am afraid that this is a fault that I have had all my life, which
has prevented me from becoming a real expert on anything or
from contributing something to the sum of positive
knowledge.

Doctor Johnson quotes the most penetrating remark (by
Dryden) ever made about Shakespeare: 'He needed not the
spectacles of books to read nature.' Indeed, book-learning,
when of a scholastic nature, can impede the acquisition of real
knowledge, as illustrated by the difference in the quality of the
clinical observations made by Shakespeare and those made by
his medically-qualified and educated son-in-law, Dr John
Hall, in his book *Select Observations on English Bodies of Eminent
Persons in Desperate Diseases*, in which all is seen through the lens
of defunct medical theory.

I have more than one copy of Johnson's *Preface*, including
that in *Eighteenth Century Essays on Shakespeare* edited by Nicol
Smith, published in 1903. I bought this volume partly because
of the neat and fastidious inscription on the flyleaf. It looks
scholarly, perhaps even pedantic, though I might be accused
of graphological overinterpretation. *Stanislaw Kryński*, it says,
Exeter College, Oxford, październik [October] *1944*.

October 1944: what a time for a Pole to be in Oxford! I
sensed at once that a man with so distinguished a hand would
have left a trace in *Wikipedia*, and so it turned out, although
only in Polish. He was born in Warsaw in 1912 and died there
in 1967. He was a philologist, literary critic and translator of
Wordsworth, Coleridge, Southey, Burns, Samuel Butler (the

author of *Hudibras*, not of *Erewhon*), and Edward Gibbon into Polish. He graduated in law from the University of Warsaw in 1934 and with a master's degree in philosophy in 1938. He also pursued a three-year course in French law, obtaining a certificate from the University of Paris. His doctoral thesis was interrupted by the war and never completed.

My copy of the book must have been as peripatetic as Kryński himself. On the rear pastedown is a sticker from a second-hand bookshop in Warsaw, evidently (from the quality of the printing, or lack of it) from the communist era. I bought the book in Paris: so Oxford, Warsaw, Paris at the least, and it was printed in Glasgow.

Surely Kryński's life must have been a very interesting, though perhaps not a happy, one. The mere outlines are a stimulus to the imagination. How did he get to Oxford, what did he do after the war was over, why did he return to Poland, what was it like to be a translator of English in Poland during the most paranoid years of a paranoid regime? Perhaps translating the elegant (or pompous) periods of Gibbon's prose was a refuge from everyday reality. Was he a believer in that regime, or did he simply make his accommodation with it? The internet tells me that there is a philologist, also called Stanislaw Kryński, born in 1948, who teaches at a Polish university. His son? If I had a hundred lives to live instead of only one, I should attempt to learn more. As it is, I shall have to be content with my imagination.

I have mentioned that the bookseller whom I knew for forty years or more said that the pulp writers of yore wrote better than those of today. True or not, Algernon Blackwood (1869 – 1951) certainly did. He had both an aristocratic and an evangelical Christian background: and, detesting the latter, he was soon attracted to eastern mysticism. Reacting against one species of untruth does not necessarily immunise one against another, and Blackwood swallowed Blavatsky, Ouspensky and Gurdijeff whole. However, he also had a rackety early life, for example exploring, if not always voluntarily, the lower depths of New York at the end of the nineteenth century. He was a man of the world, as well as of the other world.

His stories — he was immensely prolific — are often written in the upper-class diction of a man relating a story to a friend after a dinner in which much claret has been consumed, the cigar smoke swirling around one's head, as it were. His powers of description are admirable and from the first create an atmosphere of foreboding, appropriately enough for a writer about the supernatural:

> Some nights are merely dark, others are dark in a suggestive way as though something ominous, mysterious is going to happen.

Darkness, the paucity or absence of light, *does* seem to have different qualities, though a mere absence should not. Again, he writes of a house:

> It belonged to the category of unlovely houses about which an ugly superstition clings, one reason being, perhaps, its inability to inspire interest in itself without assistance.

His observations of human affairs are acute and often ironical:

> The vitality of old governesses deserves an explanatory memorandum by a good physiologist. It is remarkable. They tend to survive the grown-up married men and women they once taught as children. They hang on for ever, as a man might put it crudely...

Describing the terror of one of his characters (Madame Jodzba), he writes:

> Making no audible sound, she screamed in her mind.

Is that not a brilliant evocation of paralysis through fear?

His short story *First Hate* interested me because, though I recognise the force of that emotion and its tendency to be long-lasting, I have no great capacity for it myself. This is not because I am morally superior to it but because it requires energy and persistence to maintain, which I lack. There are, no doubt, great haters by temperament.

First Hate is one of Blackwood's after-dinner stories:

> They had been shooting all day: the weather had been perfect and the powder straight, so that when they assembled in the smoking-room after dinner they were well-pleased with themselves. From discussing the day's sport and the weather outlook, the concertation drifted to other, though still cognate, fields. Lawson, the crack shot of the party, mentioned the instinctive recognition all animals feel for their natural enemies, and gave

several instances in which he tested it – tame rats with a ferret, birds with a snake, and so forth.

'Even after being domesticated for generations,' he said, 'they recognise their natural enemy at once by instinct, an enemy they have never seen before. It's infallible. They know instantly.'

'Undoubtedly,' came a voice from the corner chair, 'and so do we.'

Note, *en passant*, that this writer of popular, not to say pulp, fiction, assumes sufficient literacy in his audience for it to understand an expression such as 'cognate fields'.

The man who interjects is called Ericssen, and he proceeds to illustrate the point with a story. At his club was a man called Hazel to whom he not only took an instant dislike (and surely we have all experienced instant antipathy to someone we have never met before without knowing quite why) but whom he recognised at once as a mortal enemy. Though for no 'rational' reason, their enmity was entirely reciprocal. They realised instantaneously that they would kill each other without hesitation if the opportunity to do so with impunity ever arose.

Years later, Ericssen was on a hunting expedition in western Canada. During this expedition, he and his guide had an accident from which only two cartridges were rescued. They were hunting elk in the wilderness when suddenly Ericssen felt that he was being watched by a malevolent creature, one that meant him ill. This uncanny feeling grew stronger until suddenly he saw Hazel who was also out hunting with a guide. Hazel did not see him at first, but in levelling his gun, Ericssen waited: he wanted Hazel to know that he was going to be shot, but also felt that it would be unchivalrous merely to kill him without having given him the chance to defend himself. When Hazel saw Ericssen, he levelled his gun at him, shot and missed. Ericssen then shot him through his head — and his guide with the second of the cartridges.

It is, perhaps, indicative of the morality of the time in which Blackwood wrote that killing the guide, an Indian (as he would then have been called) posed no problem for him, though all that he had done wrong was to have been hired by Hazel.

The story put me in mind of my one and only big game hunting expedition. I was a rather reluctant hunter, as the last thing that comes into my head whenever I see a wild animal or bird is the desire to shoot it — unless, of course, it be a crocodile running towards me. My one hunting expedition was in the Tanganyikan bush. Not long after its start, the two senior members of the expedition had a terrible quarrel and separated, one with the gun and the other with the cartridges. I accompanied the man with the cartridges: and the most we could have done, on seeing any animal, was to have thrown cartridges at it. In fact, we caught sight of one or two gazelle and some wild dogs, an unattractive species of canine and now rare and endangered. I was pleased that we had no means of shooting them.

Eventually the two senior members of the expedition reunited and reconciled. It was late in the day, and they felt guilty towards me because I had been deprived of the opportunity of killing something. We came across a little green snake at the base of a tree, and they insisted that I shoot it so that the day's hunting should not have been entirely in vain. I took aim and shot. When the smoke cleared, the snake was gone — vapourised, I suppose. I felt no sense of satisfaction, rather the reverse. The snake may have been a green mamba, a highly venomous species but not dangerous to man because it is mostly arboreal and very rarely gets to bite him. What I regret is not having had the moral courage to refuse to shoot it for no good reason, even though the social pressure to do so was very slight by comparison with that in, say, a war.

It seems to me odd that Blackwood, attracted to eastern religion and mystical belief, was a keen hunter himself and saw no contradiction between the two. But consistency is not part of human nature.

Incredible as it now seems to me, and a sign of the loss of individual liberty in the intervening fifty-six years, I was permitted by my parents to hitch-hike round France in the company of a French penfriend when we were sixteen years old. My parents' anxiety about it, if they felt any, could hardly have been incapacitating: not that I considered it for a moment, any more than I did twenty years later when I crossed Africa by public transport from Zanzibar to Timbuktu. Not anxious on my own behalf, I could hardly imagine anyone being so either.

On that earlier journey through France, we were given a lift by a monk on his way back to his monastery, where he offered to put us up for the night. This was a luxury for us, for we had otherwise pitched our tent by the side of a small road (*camping sauvage*, camping outside a designated site, was not then frowned upon, let alone illegal), and in those days tents were simple affairs, very uncomfortable, the stones coming up through the groundsheet and the rain coming through the canvas if so much as touched. Nowadays, tents are almost palatial: it is as if we have abandoned liberty for comfort.

I am afraid I was too callow a youth to have taken much interest in the monastic life. As far as I was concerned, there was no God and that was the end of it. Those who spent their lives in the service of the non-existent were fools, harmless and perhaps even nice, but fools nonetheless. There was, moreover, another reason why I took no interest in the monks' way of life: I was at an age when an infinite time seemed to stretch before me, such that if, by chance, I developed an interest in something later, there would be time enough to study it. Moreover, I assumed that the monastic way of life, having existed for hundreds of years, would continue to exist, and therefore there was no hurry to study it. I had no idea that the way of life was in the process of disappearance, that the monks were, in their way, the Tasmanian tigers of our time, almost the last of their kind.

The one thing that I remember from my brief stay was how jolly, to my surprise, were the monks. I had assumed that they would be taciturn, solemn and gloomy, even if they were not members of a silent order, but I was utterly mistaken: the monks laughed a lot and seemed more than content with their lot. They were as happy as any group of people I had encountered. Ever since, I have not considered the monastic or conventual way of life as sad or escapist.

Nuns, at least in Europe, have become vanishingly rare. A few years ago, I visited a convent in Flanders founded more than eight centuries earlier and which, in the 1970s, had moved into modern premises, comparatively not-ugly considering the date of construction. The convent at the time seemed still to have a future, but when I visited it, the few nuns left were ancient and would not be replaced. Again, one had the feeling of observing a species in the process of extinction. There was a small cemetery in the grounds of the new convent, and I noticed that practically all the nuns buried there had died at an extreme old age, mostly more than ninety. Being a nun is good for the health, it seems, though I doubt that anyone would take up the way of life on that account, even though health and safety have far overtaken hope and charity as virtues. Perhaps faith is necessary to the longevity of nuns.

In his book, *A Time to Keep Silence*, in which the writer Patrick Leigh Fermor described his time in the then flourishing Benedictine abbey of St Wandrille de Fontanelle, he says that he was deeply moved by the monastic life that he witnesses, though he shared none of the religious beliefs behind it:

> I am not sure what those feelings amount to, but they are deeper than mere interest and curiosity, and more important than the pleasure an historian or aesthete finds in ancient buildings and liturgy; for I have seen the former in many places and the latter – though seldom, perhaps, as well-performed as at St Wandrille – I had always known... More important was the discovery of a capacity for solitude and... for the recollectedness and clarity of spirit that accompany the silent monastic life.

Leigh Fermor had difficulty at first adjusting to monastic life, though no religious duties were imposed on him. But after some time in the monastery, he had even more difficulty in readjusting to life outside. He now found life 'an inferno of noise and vulgarity entirely populated by bounders and sluts and crooks': and that was in 1957, an epoch that we now consider as one of comparative restraint and good order. Vulgarity! Sluts! Leigh Fermor hadn't seen anything yet.

There is undoubtedly an hostility towards monks and nuns in modern society, irrespective of what they do or how they are: probably, they are felt as a silent reproach to our way of life. At any rate, I once wrote a short article in which, having disavowed religious belief, I said that the nuns in Africa whom I had met — Swiss, Irish and Spanish — were among the finest or best people known to me; and to my surprise, this provoked an outpouring of hatred directed not at me, but at monks and nuns. No doubt some of this hatred arose because of personal experience of monks or nuns who taught the writers of the letters (there were still letters in those days), but I think there was more to it than that. It was that monastic life itself, even a partial retirement from or renunciation of the world, was, in the words of Leigh Fermor, 'utterly remote from every tendency of modern secular thought'. As it happens, I re-read *A Time to Keep Silence* in the silent coach of a British train in which it was quite clear that most passengers had no idea of what silence is, and indeed made noise as if chasing it away as an evil demon. Silence not only throws us back on our own thoughts but is a reproach to noise, as contemplation is to the desire for constant stimulation. And in that reproach, we sense a superiority — real, not merely assumed.

Why do I lament the passing of monasticism if I have no religious feeling myself? Partly it is the loss of an ancient tradition, sorrowful in itself, but mostly because it represents the triumph of the increasing, crude monoculture of our times, all the worse because it so falsely claims to value diversity. I want there to be at least the possibility of monasticism, even if, despite certain monkish tendencies, I could never be a monk myself.

John Collings Squire (1884 – 1958) was once very famous, at least in literary circles, though he was despised by T.S. Eliot and Virginia Woolf, who thought him philistine, and is now almost completely forgotten. He was actually a good minor poet himself and in 1916 published the first book of anti-war poetry, though he was never himself at the front. He had little time for writing that was difficult or impossible to understand and had sympathy for the reader 'who does not regard art as the best means of producing a headache,' as he put in his mainly laudatory contemporary review of Katherine Mansfield's book, *Bliss and Other Stories* (it is much easier to recognise writing that has lasted than writing that will last).

At the risk of appearing philistine myself, I admit that I have some sympathy with Squire's view, which was also that of A.E. Housman, who said, in his lecture on poetry (the only one, as far as I can tell, that he gave):

Experience has taught me, when I am shaving of a morning, to keep watch over my thoughts, because, if a line of poetry strays into my memory, my skin bristles so that the razor causes a cut. This particular symptom is accompanied by a shiver down the spine; there is another which consists of a stricture of the throat and a precipitation of water to the eyes; and there is a third which I can only describe by borrowing a phrase from one of Keats's last letters, where he says, speaking of Fanny Brawne, 'everything that reminds me of her goes through me like a spear.' The seat of the sensation is the pit of the stomach.

This is not to say, of course, that poetry (or any other art) must yield its entire meaning on first acquaintance, indeed the opposite would rather be the case, but that it must have some emotional impact on first acquaintance and not be a merely intellectual puzzle such as that offered by Sumerian clay tablets.

Squire was a literary journalist whose monthly, the *London Mercury*, welcomed to its pages many of the greatest writers of the day. He was a founder of the Fabian Society and (like Bernard Shaw and many others) was attracted to Mussolini for a time. In later years, he declined into lugubrious alcoholism.

I knew nothing of him until one day I opened a book of his, written under his sometime pseudonym of Solomon Eagle, and found it very amusing. No doubt it is a waste of time to read literary journalism a century old, but I find it a pleasant pastime and it is surely harmless — except for those who count opportunity cost as a positive harm. I have since bought a few of his books in a desultory manner, among them *Books Reviewed*, published exactly a hundred years ago as I write this.

It consists of thirty-eight short essays perfectly calculated for reading while the kettle boils or the toast pops up from the toaster.

He had an excellent and fluent style and often puts things with a kind of just finality. Reviewing a volume of John Clare's poetry, edited by Edmund Blunden, he praised both the poet and editor and points out that the latter has chosen one hundred and fifty poems of two thousand known to exist. He writes:

> … an edition of him [Clare] in ten volumes would be a monument not to his genius but to an admirer's folly.

In other words, let us keep things in proportion, the most elementary and difficult of intellectual operations.

Squires' little essay on W.E. Henley (now known, if at all, for a poem that he never called *Invictus*, 'I am the master of my fate,/ I am the captain of my soul') might have been autobiography, for Henley was, like Squire, a literary editor, a minor poet and a writer of short literary essays:

> … an editor's reputation is a brief one. He may perform great services to literature in general and to particular authors, but no sooner has his last number appeared than his authors sail off on their own adventures, and his enterprise becomes a memory fading daily.

Feeling slightly guilty at wasting my time, albeit agreeably, on such a volume, I persuaded myself that I had not *really* been wasting my time when I had gleaned such gems as a quotation of William James' letters, as quoted by Squire: 'My first act of free will shall be to believe in free will', and 'The human, as distinguished from the German, mind'. Of Ernest Renan he wrote, 'He levitated at last to his true level of superficiality, emancipating himself from layer after layer of the inhibitions into which he was born…' If it is worth remembering the good things that others have said, I had not wasted my time entirely.

Squire could be very funny, not a characteristic universal among literary critics. For example, reviewing a book by Swinburne's great friend, Theodore Watts-Dunton, which revealed details of the poet's life, he wrote:

> The size of Swinburne's feet [once thought to have been exceptionally small] is now ascertained once and for all, and and it will be impossible for any future critic, however revolutionary, to reopen the question of the kind of soap he used in the bath.

Or again, reviewing a book titled *The Glands Regulating Personality* by Dr Louis Berman, the kind of book, he said, that he would not normally review, he wrote:

> … finding the phrase "A man's chief gift to his children is internal secretion composition" I knew I must go through with it. Here, beyond doubt, was one of those men with an explanation, satisfactory to himself, of everything that exists.

There are many hilarious passages in this review, but I will quote only one:

He uses Mr Strachey's account of Florence Nightingale for a ruthless analysis of the glands that made her what she was; Caesar, Napoleon, and Nietzsche are other of his specimens. He regrets that they did not live later, so that science could have rectified them.

Then there is his essay titled *The Book-Collector* about an American who 'is not by American standards a collector of the first rank'. He is a comparatively modest man but:

> The fact is he has a passion for possessing little fragments of people's lives, an interest in relics, anecdotes, glimpses of character... It is, *au fond*, the same passion as that which led the reverent Mayor to frame and glaze the butt-end of the cigar which King Edward had thrown on the station platform, and the piece of toast in which the Royal teeth had made a semi-circular indentation.

As it happens, my copy of *Books Reviewed* is inscribed by *Jack* to *Mother* – by Jack Squire, that is. I suppose I too have a passion for possessing little fragments of people's lives, or of some people's lives, and it is curious how much pleasure such an inscription gives me, though (or because) I cannot explain it rationally. As to how the book came into my hands via Squire's mother, who died in 1932, I have no idea. I cannot even make an informed guess.

Lying on the grass one day round the church in front of my house (the tombstones having long been removed as a hazard to health and safety which, as I have mentioned, are the hope and charity of our age), under what Rupert Brooke called an English heaven, reading *New Poems 1952*, an anthology of poems written in the previous twelve months, I heard a passing schoolboy say to another, 'We'll self-harm each other.'

My heart leapt with joy at this wonderfully oxymoronic but not meaningless sentence, a small manifestation of unconscious linguistic genius. Self-harm each other! It brought to mind a case when I was still practising medicine in a prison. A prisoner had self-harmed his cell-mate to death by forcing him to commit suicide by hanging himself or have his throat cut if he did not.

The anthology begins with an introduction by the great historian, C.V. Wedgwood. The anthology, she writes, 'is in itself a credit to an age, and a virtue in it, for to have many poets is the pre-essential for having good poets.' Of course, a necessary is not also a sufficient condition, and I suppose it would be possible to have many poets without a single good one. But the standard of the poems in this anthology was high, I thought, and I even knew two of them, Dylan Thomas's *Over Sir John's Hill* and James Kirkup's *A Correct Compassion*.

The very title of the latter poem throws down a gauntlet to our current moral sensibility, for a *correct* compassion implies the possibility of an *incorrect* one, and surely no compassion can ever be incorrect? The poem is dedicated to Mr Philip Allison, 'after watching him perform a Mitral Stenosis Valvulotomy in the General Infirmary at Leeds': the surgeon, Mr Allison, subsequently being appointed professor of surgery in Oxford and dying in 1974, aged only 66.

In 1952, when the poem was written, heart surgery was in

its infancy and to perform successfully even the slightest procedure on this most essential organ seemed almost miraculous. The poem is frankly hero-worshipping, but not in a sentimental or unctuous way. It begins:

Cleanly, sir, you went to the core of the matter.
Using the purest kind of wit, a balance of belief and art,
You with a curious nervous elegance laid bare
The root of life, and put your finger on the beating heart.

At the end of the operation (and the poem), Mr Allison says that he does not stitch up the pericardium because it is not necessary to do so:

For this is imagination's other place,
Where only necessary things are done, with the supreme
and grave
Dexterity that ignores technique; with proper grace
Informing a correct compassion, that performs its love,
and makes it live.

Compassion, then, is disciplined rather than incontinent, useful and necessary when accompanied or tempered by knowledge and skill, but not otherwise, when it is pure emotion. The phrase 'Dexterity that ignores technique' does not seem quite right to me, however. Dexterity is part of technique, and technique is obviously necessary in such an operation. What I think Kirkup meant was dexterity that ignored flamboyance, that was not exercised for its own sake or to impress others. But even Homer nodded.

A poem in the anthology that I did not know, by a poet of whom I had not heard (ignorance is always infinite, knowledge circumscribed) was an elegy for a lost submarine, HMS Affray, that sank near the island of Alderney, on 16th April, 1951, with the loss of all 75 men aboard. The poet was Ewart Milne, a somewhat stormy petrel who, like many another, became more conservative with age.

> Night of black depthless depths, long, long night,
> Your waters will not divide again,
> Nor her keen bisecting sides play dolphin, surfacing!

The poem was written when the wreck had not yet been located and captures well the anxious bleakness of the search for survivors:

> The face on the sea's cold mirror is our own.
> Sending out the supersonic signals,
> Searching the wide reaches for a marker buoy,
> The wide channel for a patch of oil,
> The hours tick on and men do not look at one another:
> The divers sit beside their helmets,
> The seahawks circle and make no sign,
> The telephonists are mute…
> And the second day was like an eternity,
> Like a terrible evening that would never end…

It is a fine observation that men involved in an attempted rescue do not look at one another for fear of communicating their helplessness, and again that the mind turns away from imagining what it was like to die in this way:

> In this ship, in this one-purpose hull of death,
> Was enacted this scarcely imaginable trapped horror
> Before which the mind fails, where the spirit cannot
> enter!

The scarcely imaginable trapped horror is not good poetry —
that's an ill phrase, a vile phrase, as Polonius would have put
it — but it does accurately impart our reaction to such an
event.

At the end of the poem, Milne draws a pacifist conclusion,
The submarine will soon be replaced by another, 'Death on a
voyage of death,' whose whole purpose is to inflict death:

> Listen only to the bell, listen and repeat:
> 'This is the ship that takes our sons, our lovers,
> 'And returns them from when they came'
> Over and over;
> That the child may learn it in time, in time.[25]

After every disaster, after every mass killing, after every war,
after every genocide (or attempted genocide, for genocide is
rarely successful), we say *Nunca más, nunca más!*, never again,
never again! But there is always an again.

The Russians, incidentally, spread the rumour that HMS

---

[25] Milne overlooks the possibility that the purpose of the submarine
was to keep the peace: for history suggests that he who wants peace
must prepare for war. Alas, such preparedness is no guarantee
either.

Affray sank because of a mutiny on board.

Walking down a narrow street the other day, I was surprised to see striding towards me a man whom I thought had died more than seventy years ago: George Bernard Shaw. When I was between 11 and 12, I had a teacher whom I much admired, who himself was an uncritical admirer of Shaw: and wishing to earn his approbation, and even to imitate him, I too became an uncritical admirer of Shaw. My admiration lasted for five or so years, and there is no doubt that Shaw was perfectly suited to earning the admiration of an adolescent boy, for whom shocking one's elders is the highest good.

I thought that Shaw's prose style in the long prefaces that he wrote to his plays was the acme of prose styles, and I hoped one day to imitate it. Returning to Shaw in my years of maturity, I find him an intolerable, long-winded bore, though with considerable flashes of wit. His manner of argument strikes me as undisciplined and unscrupulous, that of a man who prefers at all costs a *bon mot* to the truth, who repeatedly takes the part rhetorically for the whole and whose judgment is often unsound because he is so anxious to take people aback. No man who demanded scepticism of others was ever surer of himself, to the extent of knowing the future as if it had already happened. Here is what he wrote in 1931 in the preface to *Too True to Be Good*:

> Stalin and Mussolini are the most responsible statemen in Europe because they have no hold on their places except their efficiency; and their authority is

consequently greater than that of any of the monarchs, presidents, and prime ministers who have to deal with them... [Stalin] is no richer than his neighbours, who can "better himself" only by bettering them, not by buttering them up like a British demagogue.

The year before, in the preface to *The Apple Cart*, he had written:

Had we not better teach our children to be better citizens than ourselves? We are not doing that at present. The Russians *are*. That is my last word. Think it over.

Little Pavlik was raised to the Soviet pantheon two years later. *He* was the better citizen of whom Shaw spoke. As far as I am aware, Shaw never changed his opinion or acknowledged his mistake: he was not the type.

Shaw's *modus operandi* is evident in what is probably the most famous of his prefaces, that to *The Doctor's Dilemma*. What he does is the following: he makes a witty observation of a partial truth, and then treats it as if it were the whole truth. The partial truth in this case is that doctors sometimes act in their pecuniary interests (unlike playwrights, for example):

That any sane nation, having observed that you could provide for the supply of bread by giving bakers a pecuniary interest in baking for you, should go on to give a surgeon a pecuniary interest in cutting off your leg, is enough to make me despair of political humanity.

He goes on to say that 'the surgeon... retains his self-respect more easily [than other types of doctor]. No man who is occupied in doing a very difficult thing, and doing it very well, ever loses his self-respect... but the man who does evil skilfully, energetically, masterfully, grows prouder and bolder at every crime.'

That there have been, and no doubt are, corrupt or wicked surgeons is, alas, true; but to say as much is to lament human nature, which has many mansions. But to assert that *all* or the majority of surgeons are corrupt or wicked in this way is a grotesque libel and was such in Shaw's own day.

Shaw says things such as 'The test which the methods of treatment are finally brought is whether they are lucrative to doctors or not.' 'Treat every death as a possible and, under the present system, a probable murder... and execute the doctor, *as* a doctor, by striking him off the register.' 'According to vivisectionist logic our builders would be justified in providing artificial earthquakes with dynamite, and our admirals in contriving catastrophes at naval manoeuvres, in order to follow the line of research thus accidentally discovered.'

This constant stream of overconfident, subversive hyperbole delights and impresses a 15-year-old but exasperates someone who has experience of the intractability of life. 'The vivisector,' says Shaw, 'is actuated principally by a lust for cruelty', and it is certainly true that millions of animals have been sacrificed for experiments that prove nothing, let alone something useful. But in the little town in France near which I live, Les Vans, was born Léopold Ollier, one of the greatest orthopaedic surgeons of the nineteenth century. By means of animal experimentation, he discovered that bone grew from the periosteum, and his discovery allowed him to develop bone grafts which went some way to correcting the terrible deformities of children that were common in his time, and that alleviated terrible suffering. Ollier performed his first bone grafts on rabbits, but to suggest that he did so from some sadistic pleasure in making rabbits suffer (as they must have done) is preposterous, and there is simply no evidence to support such an attribution of motive, except that it reads well, Shaw regarding it as 'a strictly scientific psychological hypothesis, which is also simple, human, obvious, and probable.'

Gadflies have a place in intellectual life, but they are dangerous when they are taken, or take themselves, for gurus.

Poetry, it has been said, is what is lost in translation: in which case, it might be supposed, there is little point in reading poetry in translation. Is poetry not 'What oft was said, but ne'er so well express'd'? If you lose the quality of expression, you lose the value of the poetry, which otherwise contains only 'what oft was thought.'

Nevertheless, a few poets in translation still have their power to move, though whether this is due entirely to a quality in the original poetry or in that of the translation only someone equally fluent in the two languages is qualified to say.

The one and only time I was in Alexandria, I visited the house of Constantin Cavafy (or Cavafis), now — or at least then — a small museum. By the city itself, I was disappointed: any particular flavour had been dissolved in the universal solvent of architectural modernism (and highly derivative modernism at that). Cavafy's house had been well-preserved, or restored, as if left as a shrine after his death, though the cosmopolitanism of the city during his lifetime was completely of the past. There were few visitors to the museum — my wife and I the only ones that day — and an air of melancholy, entirely appropriate to the life and work of the poet, who lived as a government bureaucrat and died in 1933 without any of his subsequent renown as a poet, suffused it.

Three of his poems done into English move me in particular:[26] *The City*, *Waiting for the Barbarians*, and *Ithaca*. Although they are deeply pessimistic, yet in some fashion that I find difficult to explain or analyse, I find them consolatory, perhaps because they are warnings against, or remedies for, false and facile hope (optimists are more inclined to depression, perhaps than pessimists, who have at least the consolation of being able to say, 'I told you so.')

The City's theme is an ancient one. Horace remarked two millennia ago that travellers change their skies,[27] not their souls, who run across the sea, and Cavafy says exactly the same, though whether better, worse or equally well-expressed, I leave it to others to decide:

You say, 'I'll go to another country, go to another shore,

---

[26] Though I have no Greek, when a Greek Cypriot friend read them in Greek, I recognised their musicality.

[27] A collection of Norman Lewis's travel essays is titled *The Changing Sky*.

Find another city better than this…'

The purpose of the journey is to change your life for the better, to overcome its defeats, to repair its mistakes, to be born again, to use an evangelical Christian term. But it is all futile:

You won't find another country, you won't find another
Shore.
This city will always follow you…
Don't hope for things elsewhere:
There's no ship for you, no road.

Caminante, no hay camino.

Another poet in translation who has moved me is Miroslav Holub. He was a Czech immunologist and pathologist, who lived under the Nazi occupation and then, for much longer, under communism, neither conducive to lyrical or romantic poetising. One might say the same of the practice of pathology, especially in the phase that deals with corpses. A friend of mine alerted me to the existence of Holub more than fifty years ago (I can hardly believe the swiftness of the passage of time) from his poem then recently published for the first time in English:

Here in the Lord's bosom rest
the tongues of beggars,
the lungs of generals,
the eyes of informers,
the skin of martyrs,

in the absolute
of the microscope's lenses.

I leaf through Old Testament slices of liver,
in the white monuments of brain I read
the hieroglyphs
of decay.

This, too, is an old trope, the existential unity of Mankind in death, life having been full of sound and fury but ending in a post-mortem.

For many years, Holub was not allowed to publish in Czechoslovakia and said that none of his readers could read Czech, the language in which he wrote, only in the languages into which his poems were translated. Not surprisingly, one of his themes was the falsity in which everyone in his country was obliged to live. He has a poem titled *Kuru, or the Smiling Death Syndrome*, kuru being the neurological disease that the Fore people of New Guinea used to contract in the days when their custom was to eat the brains of their deceased relatives. This disease, caused by a sub-viral particle, was characterised by, among other symptoms, fatuous laughter, as if the sufferer were highly amused:

We aren't the Fore of New Guinea,
we don't indulge in ritual cannibalism...

We just smile,
embarrassed, we smile,
embarrassed, we smile,

embarrassed we smile.

Metaphorically, and in an ironical sense, 'we', the Czechs, *do indulge, or have indulged in*, ritual cannibalism, for what else were the show trials of Slansky and the eleven others executed for phantom political crime, other than ritual cannibalism (the executed were all communists themselves).

Holub wrote Aesopically: even so he was not published, so in a sense he didn't have to write in this fashion since he wasn't published anyway. But an Aesopian approach, that leaves something for the reader to do, is always more effective than a direct harangue. Some of the lines in *Punch's Dream* seemed especially powerful to me, for personal reasons. In the poem, Holub implies that people under the regime are but puppets with no real agency of their own. But one of the rebellious puppets says:

> ...before the puppeteer knows what's happening
> I'll speak in my own voice,
> you know, my own voice,
> out of my own head...

This could not but remind me of my one and only visit to North Korea, now more than thirty years ago, in the reign of Kim the First. I was crossing the huge open space before the Great People's Study House, an architectural amalgam of pagoda and fascist mausoleum, which was utterly deserted except for a lone young North Korean, at first in the distance, and me.[28]

As we passed each other, he asked me, *sotto voce*:

'Do you speak English?'

'Yes,' I replied.

'I am a student of the Foreign Languages Institute,' he continued. 'Reading Dickens and Shakespeare is the greatest, the only, joy of my life.'

Our conversation lasted only a few seconds before we parted: he was already risking a great deal by so speaking. I think I grasped what he meant, however. In Dickens and Shakespeare, the poorest, most oppressed or despised person at least speaks in his own voice, in his own words, something which no North Korean is permitted to do.[29] Having been born into this silence, what a revelation Dickens and Shakespeare must have been. As Holub put it:

> I'll speak in my own voice,
> you know,
> my own voice,
> out of my own head.

When I was a very small boy, my father had a factory in

---

[28] It was the kind of space in which a crowd (in contradistinction to an organised mass or parade of the kind the North Korean regime specialises in) would be a revolution, as Custine puts it in his *Russia in 1839*.

[29] Even Abhorson, the condemned man in *Measure for Measure*, waiting for execution, says 'I will not be hanged today' — and means it.

Tonypandy in the Rhondda. He would go there for days at a time when Wales seemed very distant. Once he took me with him — this was well before the motorway in Britain — and the journey seemed endless. I remember very little of Tonypandy, except that the factory was ramshackle and everything in the town seemed sooty black. The mountains, the slagheaps, the streets, the houses, the sky, the grass, even the rain, were black, the latter causing everything to glisten malevolently. Sometime later, my father moved his factory to the relatively salubrious Caerphilly, and I never went to Tonypandy again. Goodness knows what it is like now.

The name of the town still exerts a fascination for me for the above autobiographical reason. The unjustly neglected writer, Rhys Davies, was born there, or in a village adjacent to it without a gap, and the poet, Idris Davies, wrote a long poem with the title *Tonypandy*, which he used for a slim volume of his poems.

Idris Davies (1905 – 1953) is to me a very sympathetic figure. He was quietly remarkable. Modest to a fault, spending seven years at the coal face between the ages of fourteen and twenty-one, then three years unemployed, originally Welsh-speaking, he crawled up the educational ladder, as did so many other Welsh miners, by painful and strenuous efforts, and qualified as a primary school teacher, moving to London before becoming a poet praised by T.S. Eliot. He thought of himself as a failure, as only a minor poet (as indeed he was). But that he was a poet of any distinction at all was remarkable. He would have liked to teach at a higher level than primary school but never did. In his diary he wrote, piercingly:

> I feel very unsatisfied with my progress. I've spent eight of these years in London – from 1932 to 1939 – and what have I done there, outside my daily work? Nothing or very little. A few poems published here and there, a diploma in history, and a small book in 1938. No wife, no lectureship: too shy to get one; too slow to get the other.

A sense of failure is a widespread or a common sentiment, and to me an attractive one, far more attractive than an awareness of having triumphed in life. But I do not consider Davies a failure.

Tonypandy, the poem, apostrophises the archetypal South Wales miner, Dai Bach, or Little Dai. (*Bach* is a friendly term of address in Wales, beautiful in my view, and I am always delighted to be addressed as such when I am in Wales). The poem begins:

> Dai bach, Dai bach, with your woollen muffler
> Tight around your strong dark neck,
> Why do you seem so sad and lonely
> There at the corner of Pandy Square,
> Was it the moist grey hour of twilight?

The poem goes on to tell how it was, or seemed, natural for Dai, as it had been for Idris, to do down the mine as soon as he was old enough to do so:

> And the pride you had in your father's
> Loins and shoulders when he bent

Between the tub and the fire,
And the days you counted, counted, counted,
Before you should work in the mine.

As Iris Origo says in her autobiography, one of the difficulties of growing up (in her case in aristocratic circles) is that you have no standard of comparison. Dai, and Idris, didn't even realise that they had a choice: and without realising that, there is in fact no choice. A Rwandan peasant told the French journalist Jean Hatzfeld that in Rwanda you don't go to agriculture, agriculture comes to you. So it was in South Wales in Idris Davies' time, the harvest being coal.

He experienced the hardship of the 1920s in South Wales at first hand, hardship of an almost unimaginable intensity now, and though I believe that socialism to be a mistaken economic doctrine, it is impossible to blame Davies and those like him who lived through those times for having adopted it. Perhaps his best known volume, insofar as any of his four volumes is known, is *The Angry Summer*, about the miners' strike in 1926 and its defeat. The miners in that year continued their strike after the General Strike collapsed, and while some have condemned or at least criticised Davies' verses as too politically engaged to be real poetry, yet to me they seem authentic in their feeling and not always infelicitous in their expression. Much under the influence of Housman (whose experience of life could hardly have been more different from his own), Davies insisted that his poetry should speak directly to the reader. Here he writes in the voice of the unemployed miners of South Wales, tramping through the countryside in search of work, refugees from destitution:

Roses in gentlemen's gardens
Smile as we pass by the way,
And the swans of my lord are sleeping
Out of the heat of the day.

And here we come tramping and singing
Out of the valleys of strife,
Into the sunlit cornlands,
Begging the bread of life.

But Davies was an amiable and thoroughly decent man, no fanatic. The terrible suffering that he had seen (and experienced in his own flesh and blood) did not make him vengeful or wish violence on others. Towards the end of his life, he abjured politics as a realm of dangerous illusion. In his diary, he wrote:

I have met many kinds of escapists in my time. Perhaps the greatest escapists of all are fanatics, political and religious. How many extremists have I met in London and South Wales, young humourless people with a very slight or no regard for culture, but who blind themselves to the hard facts of everyday life by their fanatical worship of theory?

His long ballad-like poem, *I Was Born in Rhymney*, begins:

I was born in Rhymney
To a miner and his wife –
On a January morning

I was pulled into this life.

I cannot fully explain why, but I find the line 'I was born in Rhymney' — which, incidentally, was poorer even than the generality of such mining villages in South Wales — moving, perhaps because of its unrhetorical modesty. The poem is an autobiography, edited of course (as which autobiography, *pace* Rousseau, is not?), not devoid of humour. Here is the verse about the soap-box orators of Speakers' Corner in Hyde Park, whom Davies encountered when he came to London:

> O the orators, the orators,
> On boxes in the parks,
> They judge the Day of Judgment
> And award Jehovah marks.

Davies' life was quietly tragic. In 1951, he underwent unsuccessful surgery of cancer of the stomach and never rose from his bed again, though he died in 1953. He was an estimable man.

To describe my absence of knowledge of various subjects as lacunae would be like describing the Pacific Ocean as a puddle. And so it was that I had never heard of Dionysius Lardner (1793 – 1859) until I bought from my friend at Cosmos Books a chapter of his vast compendium, *Museum of Science and Arts*, that was devoted to railway accidents.

Lardner was a brilliant populariser of the science of his time and was temporarily extremely famous, which makes my total ignorance of him all the more regrettable. Born, raised and educated in Dublin, he moved to London where he was appointed the first professor of natural history and astronomy of London University. He had written treatises on the calculus and the steam engine and went on to become a kind of impresario of general knowledge, commissioning such authors as Walter Scott and Thomas Babington Macaulay to write for him. He was extremely interested in railways and steamships, indulging in controversies about them with Isambard Kingdom Brunel in which he came off second best. He was thought to have claimed that no steamship could ever, for purely engineering reasons, cross the Atlantic by steam alone. In fact, what he claimed was that no steamship could do so profitably, so much coal would it have to carry. For some time, this was actually the case. His book on the economics of railways was quoted by Marx and one biography of him — the only one as far as I can tell — says that he was the first to apply graphs to the problems of economics. I have no way of knowing whether this is true.

An air of charlatanism, like a faint scent, hung over or around him; he was always irregular in his ways, and in 1839, scandalously for the time, he ran off with another man's wife (the man in question beating him severely when he caught up with him in Paris). He went to America for five years, where he was a successful lecturer and showman, subsequently returning to Paris. He died in Naples where the Bourbon King of the Two Sicilies, generally regarded as a frightful reactionary, may have employed him, having been a great patron of science. Although Lardner published scores of books and must have written millions of words, he is forgotten today

— the ultimate fate, of course, of the immense majority of those who put pen to paper.

The chapter in his *Museum of Science and Arts*, published in twelve volumes in 1854, is instructive and fascinating. He begins by describing with something that appears like relish the sheer horror of train crashes and other accidents associated with the railways, such as people being killed while trying to rescue their hats as they flew out of the window (surprisingly numerous in the category of fatalities 'within [the passengers'] control'). He writes:

> The spectacle exhibited on the occasion of some great railway collisions would have been believed by our forefathers to be too extravagant even to be allowed a place in the wildest fiction. Colossal vehicles, weighing several tons, shivered to pieces; rods of iron, thick and strong enough to sustain a vast building, bent, twisted and doubled as though they were rods of wax; massive bars of metal snapped and broken like glass; bodies of the killed dispersed here and there, among the wrecks of vehicles and machinery, so mangled as to render it impossible to recognise the disjecta membrae of the same body – the countenances of the dead, where countenances remain at all, having a ghastly expression of the mingled astonishment and horror with which the sufferer was filled in the brief instants which elapsed between the catastrophe and death, the survivors, maimed and wounded, lying under the ponderous ruins, groaning in agony and supplicating for relief and extraction.

But Lardner, like any modern journalist, wants it both ways: prurience and condemnation of prurience. He goes on to point out that such accidents are extremely rare, especially by comparison with other forms of locomotion or travel: 400 deaths a year for roughly 200,000,000 passenger miles, one death for every 500,000 miles travelled. A brief and rough calculation shows me that the risk of death per passenger mile is now about a thousandth of what it was in Lardner's time, though now there are probably far more safety notices than there were then. (I don't know how much safety notices increase safety, but I suspect that it is not by much if at all. They can, however, increase anxiety. I suspect there might even be an inverse safety notice law: the less likely an accident, the more numerous the safety notices.)

Lardner points out that, while there were no fatal accidents on French railways, there were 75 fatalities from horse-drawn carriages in the Parisian region alone: yet people were far more frightened of travelling on trains. Lardner ascribes this irrationality to the fact that when trains crash many are killed at once, whereas only a few at most die in a horse-drawn carriage accident. This is a little like the distinction that Solzhenitsyn draws between the limited murderousness of Macbeth, a consequence of personal ambition alone, and the unlimited murderousness of totalitarian regimes, a consequence of an ideological schema.

Lardner was called before parliament when Brunel proposed to run a railway line from London to Bristol. This would involve running a tunnel through Box Hill that would be the longest such tunnel in the world, much longer than any other yet run. Lardner was asked whether the air in the tunnel would be dangerous while and after a train passed through it, releasing noxious gases. With admirable honesty, he said that he did not know, having no experience to guide him, though the parliamentarians badgered him to give a straight answer, yes or no.

This brought back to my mind a little trivial historical research I once did into the history of the hospital in which I was then working, the German Hospital in Dalston. In the 1840s, in the decade of which Lardner wrote, the hospital, established to treat the then very large German-speaking population in London at the time, including Marx, was, as ever, short of money. The committee wanted to sell some adjacent land to a railway company so that it could lay a track. The doctors objected: the noise and vibration would kill the 'brain cases.' The committee, mostly aristocrats or persons with aristocratic connections, disregarded them and sold the land. On the first night on which a train passed by the hospital, the doctors and the committee stood by to observe what happened to the 'brain cases': nothing, of course.

My only close personal acquaintance with a train crash was in Milton Keynes, whither I had gone to prepare a report on an imprisoned murderer. I was wating at the station for a fast train home, but it was very delayed. Naturally I and the other passengers grumbled mightily, but then we heard that it had been derailed (a word, according to none other than Dionysius Lardner, imported from the French). One person was killed in the crash, Ruth Holland, the literary editor of the *British Medical Journal* in the long-lost days when it still reviewed books, and for whom I had occasionally written a review. I had spoken to her a few times by telephone and found her very agreeable, though I had never met her in person. Her last mile was the one in 50,000,000 passenger miles that ended fatally. I can't call this a coincidence, but whatever I call it, I sometimes think of this event with sorrow. Why her, I ask myself, and not someone else whom I did not know? Of course, if it had been the latter, his or her acquaintances would have asked 'Why him, or her, and not someone else?' — and so on *ad infinitum*. Why not no one? That would have been the best, after all.

Lardner's British career was permanently ruined by his elopement with another man's wife. They were very censorious in those days, though I am not sure that we are much better now: it is just that we are censorious about other matters. All the same, Lardner had a noble obituary in the *Railway Magazine*:

> One false step… destroyed his popularity and rendered his name and his work inadmissible in decent society. We are not the apologists of Dr Lardner – far from it; but we must say, we think it rather hard that a man's private sins should be pressed into service to destroy his public utility. If that rule was general, how many of our public men, who are the first of the day, would be able to maintain their position?

Are we so much more sophisticated than our Victorian forebears?

In my experience, admittedly limited to two cases, those who murder in order to receive the proceeds of a life insurance policy do so very soon — within two weeks, in fact — of the sum assured having been drastically increased. This gives the police a clue as to motive. On the other hand, I do not know how many cases go undetected, or how many times sums assured are drastically increased. The correct statistic to know is, of those people on whose life the sum assured is drastically increased *and* who are subsequently murdered, what proportion are murdered by the beneficiaries of the life assurance? A hundred per cent would be my guess.

Sydney Henry Fox (1899 – 1930) was a petty swindler whose mother's life was insured for £3000 — the equivalent, perhaps, of £180,000 today — if she died before midnight the following day. Why an insurance company should accept such a contract, which was almost an incitement to murder, I do not know — but it did. Be that as it may, Fox's mother duly died in a fire in an hotel with ten minutes to spare, so to speak. Not surprisingly, Fox was arrested, tried, found guilty and executed. Recently, doubt has been cast on the safety of the conviction and the trustworthiness, indeed the probity, of the evidence given by the pathologist, Sir Bernard Spilsbury, at Fox's trial. Certainly, Sydney James Fox was no ornament to society, and the circumstantial evidence against him was very strong; but he was still entitled to the benefit of the doubt, the possibility of which Spilsbury was too staunch in denying.

Fox's case is the first described by Harold Dearden in his book, *Death Under the Microscope*, published in 1934.

Dearden was an interesting figure. He qualified as a doctor and served in the First World War, in which much of his work consisted of making men fit to be slaughtered and returning them to the front after they had been injured. He himself was invalided out of the Army with shell-shock, having also lost an eye. After the war he became first a psychiatrist and then a playwright and screenwriter with such success that he gave up clinical practice. He was recalled to the colours during the Second World War and ran an interrogation centre for suspected enemy spies and captured soldiers, apparently using such methods as sleep and food deprivation, the latter perhaps better called starvation. This, of course, raises questions of ends and means: does the end ever justify the means? If we answer no, we reach Kant's absurd conclusion that we should tell a murderer the whereabouts of his intended victim if he should ask us. If, on the other hand, we answer yes, we open the door to the most terrible abuses. The only solution to the dilemma is the exercise of judgment, fallible as it might be.

Dearden saw and experienced many terrible things in the Great War and no doubt this caused him to grow an emotional carapace. It was the carapace that allowed him to adopt a jocular tone in his book about murder, a tone that he shared with Anthony Berkeley Cox, aka Anthony Berkeley and Francis Iles, the great crime novelist who was also wounded in the First World War. Agatha Christie, who nursed men wounded in that war, was also often jocular about murder.

Here is Dearden on the way that Sydney Fox avoided service in the Great War:

> ... before he could possibly be sent overseas, he earned a pension for life of eight shillings a week by something in the nature of an epileptic attack, his only contribution to

the service of his country.

Fox was a good-looking boy:

> He was an admirable specimen of the "lovely boy" which
> is so irresistible to ladies of a certain age and appetite, and
> it was doubtless the charm of his manner and the vivacity
> of his conversation which made him, at the same time,
> no less sought after by gentlemen of wealth, leisure and
> unusual tastes... A married lady of middle age and
> considerable means lost her heart to him. She took a flat
> in Southsea, where Sydney and his mother went to live
> with her, and had she not been so unwise as to disclose
> the fact that she had made a will in her idol's favour, the
> three of them might have gone on for years in the
> happiest situation imaginable... It is undoubtedly one
> thing to be occasionally charming and quite another to
> be charming all the time under something of the nature
> of a contract. Sydney's duties began to bore him, and he
> could not but realize that if the lady died at once
> everything would be superb... The tap to a gas-fire in the
> lady's bedroom got turned on somehow while she was
> asleep.

She survived, and (or but) it was only when Sydney stole and
pawned some of her jewellery that her eyes were opened.

Dr Dearden is jocular about other cases too. In a chapter
titled *A Kentish Town Tea-Party*, he combines horror with
humour — possibly as a defence against all that he had seen:

Precisely what took place at that ill-omened tea-party can only be imagined. But the conclusion of it found Mrs Hogg in her neat black frock stretched on the floor of the sitting room with her head almost severed from her body. There is reason to believe that she had not lent herself to this state of affairs without some opposition... Mrs Pearcey was able to solve with a minimum of inconvenience not only the problem of what to do with Mrs Hogg, but of what to do with her baby in addition. She packed Mrs Hogg into the perambulator and placed her baby on top of her. Then, covering the whole with an antimacassar from the back of her sofa, she wheeled her ghastly load with the utmost unconcern down the front steps into the street.

There are no strictly psychiatric observations in Dr Dearden's book, but he offers some observations that could have been made by anybody. He says of a certain type of psychopath:

He [wants] everybody to be happy. But he himself must be happy first. It is the straightforward adherence of this simple rule of conduct that makes of the egoist the implacable though smiling demon he so often shows himself to be.

As Hamlet puts it, 'one may smile, and smile, and be a villain.'

Dr Dearden retired after the Second World War to Hay-on-Wye, the home town of Arthur Rowse Armstrong whom I have already mentioned, and to whom Dr Dearden devoted a chapter in his book. Interestingly, he says that Armstrong practised in Brecon, as if by premonition he did not want to besmirch the name of the town in which he was to retire with the name of a man for whom he felt absolutely no sympathy, perhaps because Armstrong, who saw none of the slaughter at the front and suffered no injuries, left the army with a higher rank than Dearden's: Major to his Captain. He ends the chapter by citing Sir Bernard Spilsbury's semi-perjured evidence at Armstrong's trial:

> … he blew the little Major as surely to perdition as could one of those shells which that pasteboard officer had so sedulously avoided in the past.

Here speaks resentment, loud and clear.

What is the importance of sincerity in literature (assuming that it can be gauged with anything like accuracy)? That insincerity is always a vice does not help us to decide, for something may be necessary without being sufficient. Indeed, sincerity in the service of something abominable is frightening, and makes the abominable all the more abominable. I think in particular of the writer and *soi-disant* philosopher, Ayn Rand, who oozed monomaniac sincerity like a secretion and who, mysteriously to me (given her deeply unattractive character) became the leader of a powerful cult. Her fiction is wooden, humourless, simplistic and interminable. She must have been one of the very few modern authors to have written an apology for rape; and her philosophy, with its worship of size, power and ruthlessness, is repellent. But she was sincere all right.

Ewart Milne (1903 – 1987) was an Irish or Anglo-Irish poet who served in the Spanish Civil War on the republican side, providing medical supplies and possibly gun-running as well. I have quoted a poem of his earlier. He never achieved any great fame, a failure that he attributed to being considered too English in Ireland and too Irish in England. (We all have our excuses and explanations for our failure.) In 1967 he published a volume of poems, *Time Stopped*, of which very few unsigned copies can be found, suggesting that he had to give the book away. It is one of the rawest documents I have ever read.

It consists of 112 poems, if I have counted them correctly, written in the eighteen months after his wife's death in 1964 at the age of 57. They form a long threnody to her death, and while their overall quality as poetry might be questioned, the sheer weight and intensity of his grief comes across and overpowers the reader.

There is more to his grief than the loss of his wife, however. After her death, on reading her papers, he discovered that an Irish poet, Patrick Galvin, twenty-four years his junior, to whom he had offered support and friendship, and who in return had long flattered him and his work, had not only had a long affair with his wife but that she had been supporting him financially for many years (she was wealthy in her own right).

There are hundreds of lines of grief, and whether or not they are poetry, or good poetry, they seem to me a sincere and truthful reflection of the author's psychic pain:

> Do not just have ceased to be
> Even if I cannot touch you

Even if I cannot reach you
Even if infinitely far away
Be somewhere. be somewhere

This is the thought of all who have suffered grievous loss, and
I think it well-expressed. Moving, too, is Ewart Milne's
awareness of his own standing as a poet, that was forced upon
him by his wife's death:

Now till my last breath is out
I must turn like a squirrel in a cage
For you carried your life's ambivalence into death
And made it mine.

I am conscious not of laurels now but trees
Bare in the wintry night of lost minor poets
Those who for all their sweat and strife
Never once struck out the blazing note
The deathless line
The sudden light on human love and life.

But there are also pages of blind rage in this book, which is
161 pages long, directed at Patrick Galvin who is depicted as
a snake in the grass, a seducer who from the first had his eye
on his wife's money. Her he absolves from guilt completely:
she is the innocent victim of Galvin's machinations rather
than a willing partner in deceit. Presumably any other attitude
would have been too painful (and humiliating) for him to have
entertained in his mind even for a moment, let alone commit
to print. He admits to having been a less than perfect husband,

not only sometimes bad-tempered and unreasonable (violent, perhaps?) but something far, far worse:

> All right I hurt you
> Hurt you falling in love with your daughter
> Though it was you in her I loved…

> All right I hurt you . tactless fool
> I never dirtied you
> I never touched her
> I never loused up our marriage
> Or our life story
> He did that . it was he…

Alive to his own pain, he seems distinctly undersensitive to that which he must have caused his wife. He calls down curses upon Patrick Galvin:

> May he burn in hell's molten fire for all his lies

He excoriates Galvin in poem after poem:

> Spawn of the monstrous mouth
> Thief of the world
> Treachery is his name

But in the last section of the book his grief is uppermost:

> I reject both life and death
> Because they gave then took away

My dear love's breath.

Time stopped, as Milne says in one of his poems, when his wife died, but he survived her by seventeen years. Did time heal, or did he continue listlessly to live because he could not die? At any rate, he published at least seven books, in addition to *Time Stopped*, after his wife's death. As for Galvin, it does not appear that he was much affected by the accusations against him in the book, which was admittedly of very limited circulation.

There is more. Milne accuses Galvin, nor surprisingly, of having been a wife-stealer, but when Milne met his wife, she was already married to someone else. Although Milne says that he did nothing to alienate her affections, this strains credulity. Clearly, however, he needs to say this if his accusations against Galvin are to stick and if we are to sympathise with him. But after Milne died and an obituary of him had been published in *The Times*, a correspondent wrote the following in response, which was published:

> His own lechery was notorious. To my wife's astonishment, he made a pass at her within 10 minutes of their first meeting; and I vividly recall his indignation and sense of ill-usage when he complained to me that, in his sixties, nubile young women rejected his amorous approaches. He attributed this to the selfishness of the younger generation.

Does this mean that all of his grief, all of his rage, all his pain, were unreal or insincere? Surely someone of his propensities could not feel genuine grief or be truly aggrieved? I do not think that this is so. Grief and rage are common to the virtuous and the vicious alike.

One last thing: Milne's wife died of lung cancer. Milne tells us that in the 1930s, she took up smoking with enthusiasm, not so much because she liked it but more as a gesture of social liberation. She died in the year, 1964, in which it was officially recognised that smoking caused lung cancer.

> In the Twenties and Thirties smoking was the in-thing
> The defiance and rebel badge . how were we to know
> That in thirty years it would bring its dark harvest home

All that tuning in, turning on, and dropping out of the 1960s now seems to be bringing its dark harvest home.

It is not surprising, perhaps, that as one grows older, one's mind becomes more allusive. After all, there is more experience for the mind to allude to; as one's personal future contracts, so one's personal past expands, or even looms. As one browses books, more and more of them seem to have something to say that is directed at oneself, and this irrespective of their other qualities. Needless to say, some books have more power to evoke than others, but their literary value may have little to do with that power or be only tangentially related to it. What one reads with emotion, another will read with indifference.

Browsing in a bookshop in Paris, as is my wont whenever I am there, I started to read a book just published titled *Le silence et le bruit: Algérie 1962, l'été où ma famille a disparu* (The Silence and the Sound: Algeria 1962, the Summer When My Family Disappeared). It was by Hélène Cohen, an actress, director and screenwriter, and it was her first book.

It is a journey into her family's hidden past. It begins when the author reads what her mother has had inscribed on her father's tombstone, adding to it the names of his father, mother, sister and brother-in-law, all of whom disappeared, never to return, in Algeria in June, 1962, *after* the signing of the Evian Accords that put an end to the Algerian war of independence. To these four were added the name of her father's youngest sister, who committed suicide one year after the surviving family had moved to France.

The events alluded to on the tombstone were never alluded to in the author's childhood. So total was the silence in this regard that the tombstone inscription was her first inkling of them. This started her twenty-year effort at recuperation and elucidation. Her efforts met with only very partial success, not only because of the natural workings of time, but because of the various interests in play, not least the French state's desire to draw a line by means of amnesia under an episode in history that was brutal and inglorious, and the Algerian state's own desire or need to deny the cruelty and criminality of its own foundational struggle. (It was indeed fortunate for France that it lost the war, politically if not militarily.)

The author's father, by temperament not talkative or emotionally expansive, became almost shut-in after the kidnap and murder of his closest relations. The author was only seven months old when this happened, and her father was to her always a distant and unemotional man who never spoke of his or of anyone else's feelings, and never spoke of the past. Yet there is a photograph of him holding up the author on a beach in Algeria when she was a baby, in which he looks as any proud and affectionate new father might.

Reading a few pages into the book was sufficient to induce me to buy it. 'I cannot help thinking,' wrote the author, 'that when we are silent, it is because we have something to hide. What was it that my father was trying to hide?' And again, 'When he spoke, it was by necessity, to organise the outside world. Most of the time, he was silent. Of feeling, emotions, never. I do not remember ever having had a single conversation with him. I do not remember an intimate or tender moment... It was just like that.'

This returned me to my own childhood. A scene in particular rose to my mind. I must have been about six or seven. I had fallen in the garden and grazed my knee. It bled and some gravel entered the wound: I bore a greyish scar for years afterwards, though there is now no trace of it. My mother held me and cleaned the wound with disinfectant but offered no words or gesture of comfort, as if the need to organise the outside world were all that counted in this situation, as if the inner world were the place that was really dangerous.

And so it was for my mother. She had been a refugee from Nazi Germany when she was nineteen and a quarter-years old and never saw her parents again. They managed to escape to China, where they died. Unlike Hélène Cohen, I always knew a little of this past, though always in the barest outline, that is to say no more than I have just written.[30] My mother never spoke of her experiences, let alone of her feelings about them. She would occasionally allude to something from before 30th January, 1933 (the date Adolf Hitler was appointed Chancellor) such as the time her father, a doctor in Berlin, was called in the middle of the night to attend to a person injured in a nearby road accident, but she never spoke of anything after 30th January, 1933, until she became secretary to Jack Jackson, a popular band leader of the time in London: and even then her accounts were sketchy to the point of being skeletal.

I knew by a kind of instinct that one did not ask her about this past: it was too painful to be evoked. There was a further reason for her locked-in quality, namely her relations with my father. Not a single word do I recall ever having passed between them in eighteen years, except one night when I woke and heard her shout at him, 'You're a wicked, wicked man!' Otherwise, the most complete silence reigned between them, a silence that was not merely the absence of sound but had a positive quality (as darkness did sometimes for Algernon Blackwood). So complete was the silence that, when I visited the home of a friend in which the adults spoke to each other, I found it strange and even disturbing.

After her death, I found the letters that her father had written to her from Germany and then Shanghai, whither he, his wife and my mother's older sister had taken refuge after applying to all the embassies in Berlin. It came as a surprise to

---

[30] My first cousin knew almost nothing of this until he was in his 70s.

me that letters reached England from Shanghai during the war, I suppose through the offices of the Red Cross. In 1942, my grandfather (whose Iron Cross won in the First World War as a medical officer I still possess) wrote, in surprisingly good English, 'It is a beautiful spring day and the sun is shining brightly, but there is no sun bright enough to penetrate the dark clouds that are covering the whole earth.' But he added that he remained hopeful that one day the clouds would clear, as indeed they did, at least for a time, and at a terrible cost. He and his wife never saw the clearing, however, for they both died in Shanghai in 1944. Her sister then wrote to her: did she want their tombstones to be in English or in German? I have little doubt, though no documentation, of which she chose.[31]

Of course, I regret my mother's silence and even more her emotionlessness in my childhood, which affected me for many years and perhaps affects me still. But I recognise that it was a defence against what could not be mended. It has always seemed to me extremely shallow and unimaginative to suppose that talking can always make the past better.

Among my mother's letters that I found after her death, and of whose existence I had no knowledge before, I found something so infamous on the part of one of her relatives, something so disgraceful about the possibilities of human nature, that I forebear from mentioning it, though it concerns only people who are now dead and who cannot therefore be harmed by the revelation. As it happens, my father also had a shameful secret about his past (as no doubt we all do) about

---

[31] After she moved to America from China, in 1948, my aunt apparently denied that she spoke German. However, on her deathbed she returned to it. My mother did not.

which he remained silent all his life. There is pain that is beyond words to express or to assuage and which can be made only worse by rehearsal.

A man on whose tomb are inscribed, at his own request, the words 'Steel true, Blade straight' might be suspected of having been a bit of a bore, but in the case of Sir Arthur Conan Doyle not only were they accurate, but they were inscribed on the tomb of a man of genius, thus refuting the common, and commonplace, idea that a genius must be tormented to the point of behaving badly.

Of course, genius also needs good luck. Unlike the person who is accidentally shot dead in the crossfire of two criminal gangs, of whom the British police spokesman is now inclined to say that he was in the wrong place at the wrong time, the genius must be born in the right place at the right time. What would someone of Mozart's gifts have become if he had been born in, say, Scunthorpe in 1980? Conan Doyle was born in the right place at the right time — for someone of his gifts and temperament. But he was not in all respects fortunate — no one is — and I do not wish to detract in the slightest from his brilliant achievement. No one is so fortunate that he need make no effort, at least not if he wants to leave something worthwhile behind him.

Although he would have been reluctant to agree, Conan Doyle will forever be remembered for Sherlock Holmes, a creation of genius even if its creator grew tired of his own creation. The stories, so easy and delightful to read, are in fact filled with wit and shrewd observation of humankind. Of

Conan Doyle it could not be said, as Holmes said of Watson, that he saw but did not observe.

I will take a single story at random to illustrate the brilliance of Conan Doyle's style, wit and perception, *The Adventure of the Illustrious Client*, one of the stories in the last collection that Conan Doyle published (in 1927), when he was 68, four years younger than I as I write this. I do not choose this story because it is the best — it assuredly is not — or because it illustrates my thesis better than any other I could have chosen; I could have chosen any other for the same purpose.

There is a kind of understanding and friendship between Holmes and Watson that is at once cool and intense, with much that is unsaid but also known. They inhabit a world, or if you like a culture, of the implicit rather than the explicit, of irony rather than of overstatement or exaggeration. The genius of Conan Doyle is to make this world or culture immediately comprehensible to those who have never shared it.

Though their friendship is intense, there remains a certain formality between Holmes and Watson. *The Adventure of the Illustrious Client* begins with Holmes telling Watson, the narrator of the story, that he has received a request from Sir James Damery for a consultation. 'I am bound to hope,' says Holmes, 'that it is not a false scent and that he has some real need for our help.'

'Our?'

'Well, if you will be so good, Watson.'

'I shall be honoured.'

This is typical of the stories: concise but conveying a great deal. The formality between Holmes and Watson, despite their long association, bespeaks a warmth and respect, rather than a coldness and distance, as we so crudely imagine nowadays that all formality of address bespeaks. And this formality put me in mind of how, when I was a young doctor, now many years ago, there were still working-class spouses who referred to each other as *Mr X* and *Mrs X.*, and never by their first names, and that such marriages were always happy and long-lasting ones.

Conan Doyle had a very realistic grasp of human relations, at least in certain respects. It is probably that, in the present circumstances of informal literary censorship, *The Adventure of the Illustrious Client* would not now be published because it contains thoughts, situations and characters that certain ideologists would find disconcerting and even heretical, however true to life they might be. Truth to life, however, is of no concern to ideologists, and certainly no defence.

The plot revolves around the determination of Violet, the supposed daughter of an eminent general, General de Merville, to marry a fiendishly wicked but handsome, charming and cultivated Austrian aristocrat, the Baron Gruner, who has murdered his first wife and several other victims but has got away with it. Violet is determined to marry against her father's will and against the advice of all the persons who care for her. Sir James Damery is supposedly acting on General de Merville's behalf, the illustrious client. Sir James tells Holmes, 'It is this daughter, this lovely innocent girl, whom we are endeavouring to save from the clutches of a fiend.' Holmes half-asked, half-asserts, that the Baron Gruner, then, must have some hold over her.

'The strongest of all holds where a woman is concerned –

the hold of love.'

A little later he adds that, 'To say that she loves him hardly expresses it. She dotes upon him, she is obsessed by him. Outside of him there is nothing on earth. She will not hear one word against him. Everything has been done to cure her of her madness, but in vain.'

She knows all about the Count's life but 'The cunning devil has told her every unsavoury public scandal of his past life, but always in such a way as to make himself out to be an innocent martyr. She absolutely accepts his version and will listen to no other.'

How many cases did I know precisely like this, of evil men who were able to persuade their lovers of their innocence!

Although he knows it in advance to be useless, Holmes decides to pay a visit to Violet in the company of the Baron's last abused mistress whom he has managed to trace, all in an effort to dissuade the young woman from taking what for her might very well be a fatal step, and certainly one that can bring her nothing but prolonged and profound misery. Of course, she will not listen to her visitors: she receives them coldly and speaks to them in a voice 'like the wind from an iceberg.'[32]

Violet says to them 'I wish you to understand once and for all that I love him and that he loves me, and that the opinion of all the world is no more to me than the twitter of those birds outside the window.'

Holmes, usually impassive, admitted to Watson that he felt 'pretty furious... for there was something indescribably

---

[32] It cannot be entirely a coincidence that Conan Doyle uses this graphic metaphor and that he had travelled to Greenland and the Arctic as a young man.

annoying in the calm aloofness and supreme self-complaisance of the woman whom we were trying to save.'

Quite so: I know, or at least once knew, how powerless suasion and logic were in the case of women in love with evil men (quite often, incidentally, not for the first time in their lives). I remember one woman, for example, who had taken an overdose because her boyfriend, in his fifties, had broken her jaw, having not long before broken her arm — or 'snapped it,' as she put it. The best beloved had not long before that come out of prison having served a sentence for having killed a previous love, and I did not think it unduly interfering of me to have warned her of the danger she was in, which it required no Sherlock Holmes-like powers to perceive. We offered her everything we could to protect her; we begged her to accept what we offered, and at last she accepted. But at the last minute she relented and walked off with the man who had broken her arm and her jaw. Never shall I forget seeing them walking down the corridor away from the hospital ward, arm in arm, as true lovers as Heloise and Abelard. This would not have surprised Conan Doyle, who *knew*: but tell it not in Gath, publish it not in the streets of Ashkalon, for it does not accord with our views.

I doubt that 'Steel true, Blade straight' could ever have been inscribed truthfully on a memorial to a near contemporary of Conan Doyle's who died fifteen years after him. I mean H.G. Wells, who was born only seven years after Conan Doyle. Both had a background in science, Conan Doyle in medicine and Wells in (mostly) biology.

Wells was born in humble circumstances, and if it is true that he had one or two lucky breaks, it was also true that he knew how to make the most of them — thanks to his genius. In very short order, he went from poverty to wealth and from social obscurity to mixing with the highest ranks of society. He knew the famous artists and writers of his day, the scientists too. He knew Freud, Einstein and Charlie Chaplin; knew Bertrand Russell, John Galsworthy, Bernard Shaw, W.B. Yeats, that last all Nobel Prize-winners for literature (he was nominated himself a number of times). He knew Prime Ministers and spoke with both Presidents Roosevelt, interviewed Lenin and Stalin, and had a string of lovers, most of them remarkable in their own way. He was a Fabian socialist, never a Marxist, who believed (theoretically) in the most absolute economic equality, though he had a huge income, kept many establishments at the same time, and always had many servants to attend to his needs. He travelled widely in luxury and had one of the most famous English architects of his day, Voysey, design and build a house for him. Oddly enough, it never occurred to him that the society that allowed him all this, starting as he did from humble beginnings, must have had some virtues and advantages, at least for someone like himself. He wanted to destroy this society, though perhaps only in the way that St Augustine wanted to be chaste. It had made possible to him a most amusing life, though this is not to decry his colossal efforts (and they really were *colossal*) to achieve it. His output was prodigious, and much of it, especially up to the First World War, of enduring value.

Although he believed that the state should be the principal

paternal parent to the child, he supported his children born out of wedlock. His family and amorous relationships were unorthodox, especially for their time, and he believed that sexual relations should be entirely free and ruled by nothing but inclination. The third volume of his autobiography, the first two of which were published in 1934, was published only in 1984, thirty-eight years after his death, having been edited by his legitimate son, G.P. Wells, a biologist who was made a Fellow of the Royal Society, the highest dignity for a British scientist, for his research on the lugworm. The third volume of the autobiography was titled *H.G. Wells in Love* and consists of accounts of his many liaisons. It is odd at first sight that Wells should have been so successful with women, for he was not very tall, his voice was inclined to be squeaky, and he had the appearance of a shipping clerk of the type who used to be awarded a gold watch after fifty years' service in the same company. He must, however, have exuded a magnetic charm.

He seems to have fascinated, and been fascinated by, women of high emotional tone, some of them (according to his descriptions) histrionic or out-and-out hysterical. He had a long affair with Rebecca West, a writer who, it seems to me, never used ten words where a thousand would do.

The third volume awaited publication for so long because the principal characters in it had to die first, so frank were its portraits of them. Particularly amusing is that of Odette Keun, daughter of the Dutch dragoman (translator and interpreter) at the Dutch legation in Constantinople. She had an exciting and varied life and wrote a number of books, most of them bad, according to Wells.

I suppose I ought to write of Odette Keun as a Bad Woman, and in a strain of resentment and hostility. She was, from certain points of view, a thoroughly nasty and detestable person, vain, noisy and weakly outrageous... She was brought up in an atmosphere of screams, recriminations and beatings. Outside the walls of the great garden [of the legation] was the Constantinople of Abdul Hamid, with its pariah dogs, its dangerous filthy streets, its chronic disposition to massacre Armenians... She ran away from home to wander in Asia Minor across the Bosporus while she was still in her teens. She was brought back and scolded by the Dutch Consul, whose face she slapped. Face-slapping among the Constantinople girls seems to have been considered a very gallant high-spirited conclusive retort to reproof... She learnt quickly, remembered brightly and never synthesised.

But although she was 'a thoroughly nasty and detestable person', albeit only from a certain point of view, Wells established her as a mistress, complete with a retinue of servants, in a house in the South of France, where he wintered with her for ten years, returning to his wife in England (whom he always called Jane, though her name was Amy Catherine) in more clement weather. Wells seemed to think that his philandering and love affairs were agreeable to his wife, to whom he wrote a moving tribute after her death; but I have some difficulty in believing that she viewed his activities with as much equanimity as he suggests. I imagine that she put up with it because not putting up with it would have been worse, and certainly being the wife of H.G. Wells would have had its compensations. Indeed, I know of a famous writer of appalling character and conduct who has a wife of the sweetest disposition. Why does she tolerate him, one asks? Because life with him has its compensations, I suppose (of the vagaries of love itself, I do not speak).

On his own account, Wells seems to have retained the affection or friendship of his lovers once their affair was over. But there is something unpleasant about his calling a mistress of ten years an 'underbred, fundamentally base and silly woman'. And he admitted that, until very late in his life, his children meant very little to him. The following sentence is rather shocking:

> The world was full of… women I had only a brief and simple use for.

Perhaps some will find this laudably frank and honest, but it is also of chilling egotism.

Wells associated his socialism with sexual freedom. Under socialism, he said, sexual relations will be more individualistic — though to judge by his own conduct, egoistic would be a better term for it. And although he claimed that the promotion of world government by a single world state was the main aim of his life and thought in grand collectivities, he never stopped to ask himself (at any rate on paper) how things would be if everyone conducted himself in these matters as he had done, especially without the means to pay for the consequences — that is to say, the great majority of mankind. Moreover, while he wanted complete sexual liberty, he also wanted the exclusive sexual possession (at least for a time) of others and admitted that he felt jealousy. These desires do not seem mutually compatible, and their incompatibility is, in fact, a powerful stimulus to conflict.

He was in many ways a deeply divided man: egalitarian and elitist, libertarian and totalitarian, optimist and pessimist. He thought the world could be made perfect by scientific organisation and yet, as *The Time Machine* demonstrates, his view of mankind in general was of the lowest.

But there is no doubt that he was a genius, not despite, but perhaps even because of, his inconsistencies.

Jean Hatzfeld, a writer whose books about the Rwandan genocide and its aftermath I greatly admire, was born in Madagascar in 1949, as was a cousin of my wife's. In 1952, Jean Hatzfeld's father, Olivier, published a little book about Madagascar in the famous series, *Que sais-je?*[33], unsurprisingly titled *Madagascar*.

Madagascar hasn't played a large part in my life, but I have long dreamed of going there. After a life in which I travelled widely, I have developed a taste for staying put, and there are now only three countries I desire to visit: Laos, Japan and Madagascar. Back in the 1990s, my wife and I booked a flight to the Red Island, as it is called, but unfortunately I had a serious reaction to the antimalarial tablets then recommended

---

[33] The series, named for Montaigne's famous sceptical question and published by the *Presses Universitaires de France*, is the French equivalent of Pelican books in Britain, devoted to a wide variety of specialist subjects for general readers.

for travel to that destination and was unable to go. When I recovered, we went on holiday to Copenhagen instead, which was very pleasant but somewhat less arduous and exciting. I suppose I shall die without having seen a lemur in the wild.

When I am in Paris, I often take the *Ligne 3* on the *Métro* in the direction of Gallieni. The latter was an army commander and first French Governor-General of Madagascar: its 'pacifier'. He exiled the native Queen of the island and in two years brought the whole island under French control, no mean feat considering its size and the obstructions to movement it presented, and still presents. Olivier Hatzfeld says, 'It was only at the cost of a hundred thousand lives that the pacification was achieved, but very quickly.' Then we read, 'The enumerated population [of Madagascar] went from 2,500,000 inhabitants in 1902 to more than 4,000,000 in 1947, which can perhaps be ascribed more to progress in the methods of counting than to a true growth in population.'

One in forty people killed or died during the 'pacification': the equivalent of 1,650,000 in the population of France today! There is nothing here to suggest dramatization for effect by Hatzfeld, France still being in control of the island when the book was published and the author evincing no particular sense of outrage at this history, as would now be obligatory to express, which was nearer to him than is the end of the Second World War to us.

Nor is this all. He mentions — he can hardly avoid mentioning — the revolt against French rule in 1947. The rebels were not supported by everyone, but 'xenophobia and paganism' were much in evidence. The revolt was not organised 'and the real chiefs of the rebel bands were the sorcerers who fanaticised the population, distributing amulets and making their troops believe that their ancestors wanted this war and would give them victory.' According to Hatzfeld, it was this fanaticism that saved French rule, for it alienated much of the population, even that part of it which desired independence.

The toll of the insurrection was terrible, for a second time in half a century. It is worth quoting Hatzfeld at some length:

> The official figure is of eighty thousand deaths. Other estimates put it higher. This number comprises European victims, some dozens of landowners, massacred during the first days, and a thousand soldiers. Among the Malgaches [Madagascans], one can distinguish:
>
> > - Men condemned and executed after a trial or summary judgment; they were not many. The most important trial, that of members of [the local] parliament, resulted in some death sentences which were commuted to life imprisonment. Six death sentences were, however, carried out in the first months of 1951; seven others, as of now, await their fate in prison.
> >
> > - Men killed during military engagements or of their wounds afterwards. Probably some thousands.
> >
> > - Men, women, and children who took to the forest, wandering, led by sorcerers, maddened by their few soldiers, dead of hunger and exhaustion. Afterwards, whole villages could not be reconstituted. These were the most numerous

victims.

- Men imprisoned or put in concentration camps from the beginning, as a preventive measure... Many died of lack of care or as a result of ill-treatment. Others were shot by mistake or accident (a train of prisoners left from Lake Alaotua and went through Moramanga; on arrival at Tananarive [Antananarivo], only the soldiers had survived.

As Hatzfeld says, 'It is useless to say that all this leaves a painful memory...' He himself, Jewish, had been deported to Germany with his wife during the war and had survived. Useless also to say how much this must have affected him, and also his son, whose subject is genocide.

In 1967, Olivier Hatzfeld published a short book titled *L'Europe, le Christ et le Monde* (Europe, Christ and the World). It was published by *Labor et Fides* in Geneva, I surmise a Protestant publisher. My copy is heavily underlined in pencil — probably a quarter of the text is underlined — and there are comments on the bottom of the page, obviously by an intelligent and educated if somewhat irascible man. He accuses the author at one point of being deeply racist, where he writes that the colonised, imitating the ways of the coloniser, 'are condemned to remain Europeans of the second class, imitators, followers; secretaries, laboratory assistants, clever servants, perhaps, but not those who open paths.'

The author [writes the former owner of the book, dating his comments 1969] is profoundly racist and ignores the time it needed for Gaul to assimilate to Roman culture.

But the note-maker was scrupulous as well as irascible. In a bubble above his note just quoted, he writes that he does not believe the author to be racist through and through. But it is interesting to see how the term *racist* was already one of the strongest condemnations more than half a century ago.

Here is another disagreement, this time about a passage in which Hatzfeld writes 'As long as the economy of a decolonised country remains dependent on foreign capital and is above all orientated towards the production of a few primary commodities, the people of this country are only the instruments of foreign wealth.' Our irritable former owner writes:

> Very exaggerated and false paragraph on the economic level. First there is a confusion between colonialism and bureaucracy. On the economic level, a 'new' country will always produce to begin with primary commodities: this is not colonialism.

In both of his books, Hatzfeld addresses the ends of life. He points out that the Madagascan peasant is not motivated by accumulation of material wealth, which makes it difficult or impossible to induce him to 'improve' his methods of production. And he says that Christian civilisation can survive only if it becomes truly Christian, that is to say generous with its wealth towards the poor of the world, ready to share it in a brotherly way, for otherwise the claims of that civilisation will simply be seen by all others as hypocritical, a mask for spoliation, domination and exploitation in practice.

The older Hatzfeld does not let on whether he had actually become a believing Christian himself, though clearly he is attracted to Christianity. Before the war, and before his deportation, he taught at a non-denominational Christian school. He must have passed his wider concerns on to his son, Jean, whose first books were about the war in Yugoslavia, after which he wrote five disturbing, appalling, magnificent and in some sense beautiful books about the Rwandan genocide.

A hundred years ago exactly (as I write this) G.K. Chesterton published his book, *Eugenics and Other Evils*. As is often the way with Chesterton, the book is a compound of unnecessary convolution, blind prejudice, mean-mindedness, and brilliant wit, analysis and prophecy. Whether you could have the peaks without the troughs I do not know; at any rate, we have what we have, and there are many writers whose works are troughs without peaks.

For brilliance of literary analysis and criticism I know nothing to equal Chesterton's passage on a verse of a music-hall song which appears towards the end of the book, on pages 170 – 175 of 188. Here is the song:

> Father's got the sack from the water works
>   For smoking of his old cherry-briar;
> Father's got the sack from the water works
>   'Cos he might set the water-works on fire.

The amount of substance that Chesterton extracts from these

four lines of a popular song without any legerdemain or false sophistication is astounding, a model that could be followed by anybody of reasonable intelligence without membership of the closed guild of literary critics.

Chesterton wrote his book at a time when eugenics, 'the idea that to breed a man like a cart-horse was the way to attain that higher civilisation, of intellectual magnanimity and sympathetic insight, which may be found in cart-horses,' was all the rage among the great, the good and the very bad. It united Swedish social democrats, Nazis, and busybodying reformers in one strain of thought, namely that if undesirable human qualities from unintelligence to criminality were hereditary, you could prevent them by forbidding those who already displayed them from reproducing themselves. Eugenics was a mixture of ignorance (as far as knowledge of genetics was concerned), disgust and impatience, the demand for a simple and easily-grasped solution to an intractable problem. As often in Chesterton's career, his main target or opponent was George Bernard Shaw — with whom he remained on very friendly terms, a relationship that would be almost unthinkable nowadays, when opinion is the measure of all things.

Naturally, Chesterton had no idea of the imminent development of genetics as a science that was to take place shortly after his death. The elucidation of the structure of DNA took place seventeen years after his death, and whether the possibility of avoiding the birth of children with terrible inborn disease on the basis of genuine genetic science (which eugenics was certainly not) would have affected his attitude can only be a matter of speculation. I suspect not, however, for when the eugenicists of his day talked of 'undesirable' children, he asked the question 'Undesirable for whom?' His answer to this question was that they were undesirable to the capitalist plutocracy and the state. Furthermore, he said, if such children were undesirable, or undesired, children were such not because of any real genetic defect but because of the appalling social conditions in which so many parents lived, conditions caused by the activities, or inactivities, of the very people or organisations that promoted eugenics.

Chesterton had an uncompromising turn of mind, not much given to grasping *on the one hand but on the other…* Everything, every new proposal, was for him the beginning of the slippery slope at the bottom of which was the *reductio ad absurdum* — or an abominable tyranny. I am not immune from this mode of thought myself, which is both an intellectual and a character flaw, though it is enjoyable insofar as it gives to those who have it a sense of their own superior penetration into the essence of things and precludes the boring necessity to think about details. Of course, slippery slopes have sometimes been slipped down, and Cassandra ought sometimes to be attended to.

Chesterton clearly hated and despised what he called 'scientific officialism'. We who have just lived through the Covid-19 pandemic are well-acquainted with scientific officialism, or perhaps I should say allegedly-scientific officialism: for the officials of the officialdom seemed often to treat science as a body of dogma rather than an openminded method of investigating reality. Their excuse for this was that *something* had to be done; their error was to think that any *something* was better than no *something*, with the corollary that doing a lot was best of all.

Chesterton was an early prophet of anti-healthism:

> It is said that the Government must safeguard the health of the community. And the moment that is said, there ceases to be a shadow of a difference between beer and tea. People can certainly spoil their health with tea or with tobacco or with twenty other things. And there is no escape for the hygienic logician except to restrain and regulate them all. If he is to control the health of the community, he must certainly control all the habits of all the citizens, and among the rest their habits in the matter of sex.

This passage fails to acknowledge ambiguity in the world or to accept that there may be such a thing (in fact, there *must* be such a thing) as judgment and a happy medium.

Let me give an example, undreamt of in Chesterton's day. There is a rare inborn error of metabolism called phenylketonuria. If a baby born with this condition is allowed to consume food containing an amino acid called phenylalanine it will become seriously handicapped for the rest of its life. If, on the other hand, it is given a diet free of that amino acid, it will live a perfectly normal life. The test for the disease is very cheap and simple and is performed on every single baby born. Would anyone really object to this, and if not, does it not suggest that health officialism is sometimes justified or even laudable?

Again, Chesterton pooh-poohs controls on tobacco. He says, of Father in the above-quoted music hall song, 'that his masters have already proved that alcohol is a poison, they may soon prove that nicotine is a poison… When I was in America, people were already "defending" tobacco. People who defend tobacco are on the road to proving that daylight is defensible, or that it is not really sinful to sneeze.'

The problem here is that your right to smoke clashes with my right not to breathe in your smoke, which is not merely unpleasant but harmful. Moreover, you expect me, whether through insurance premiums or taxes, to pay for the treatment of illnesses that are a consequence of your habit. I am fully aware that this line of thought, if carried to its logical conclusion, leads to totalitarianism, but perhaps that is more a warning against logical conclusions, which are usually bad in both directions and not just one: which I do not think that Chesterton ever really appreciated.

I arrived early one day at the cinema in the Place Saint-Michel in Paris which was showing one of those interesting foreign films from an unlikely country that attract an audience of three or four (including me). Is it a natural contrariety in me that attracts me to things that are of profoundly minority interest?

Having a little time on my hands, I walked a couple of hundred yards to a bookshop that sold cheap second-hand books, slightly grubby paperbacks displayed on trays on trestles, through which people rifle as very poor people rifle through cast-off clothes. There I came across Georges Simenon's *quand j'étais vieux* (When I Was Old). In the preface, Simenon tells us:

In 1960, 1961 and 1962, for personal reasons or for reasons I don't understand, I felt old and I began to write in notebooks.

I was approaching sixty.

I will soon be sixty-seven and it is a long time since I felt old.

I don't feel the need any further to write in these notebooks and I have given my children those I haven't used.

This, surely, is the preface of a master-writer. It explains but leaves a mystery, the mystery that is in all of us and of which there is no final understanding.

I bought the book, published in 1970 (when I was young), partly because of its smell. It was printed on rough and cheap paper, now yellowing, and I have noticed that the cheap paper of books has a national smell. I can tell from the smell alone of a book's paper whether it was published in one of the three countries whose books I buy: Britain, France and America. Of course, the smell of tobacco can overpower that of national difference. My copy of Frederick Copleston's book on Nietzsche smells to this day of old cigarettes as strongly as any ashtray, though I bought it thirty years ago. The immoderation of the smoker was, I suppose, in keeping with the subject of the book: if you take up smoking, smoke with all thy might.

I discovered that Simenon had shared my delight in notebooks, or rather that I shared his. 'From the age of seven or eight,' he writes,' I was fascinated by paper, pencils and rubbers, and a stationer's held more attraction for me than a sweet or cake shop. I loved the smell of it. Certain yellow pencils, too hard to be used in school, appeared to me more noble, more aristocratic, than any other object...' Simenon bought notebooks without knowing what he was going to write in them or use them for. I have immense quantities of notebooks bought in the same way which I probably could not fill if I wrote for twelve hours a day for the rest of my life, but if I pass a shop that sells notebooks, whether of elegance, beauty, or mere utility (that is to say, utility if I actually needed one), I invariably enter and buy. Sooner or later, this pattern of behaviour will enter the *Diagnostic and Statistical Manual of the American Psychiatric Association* in its list of disorders, no doubt giving the prevalence in the population of the strange compulsion to accumulate unneeded notebooks.

When I Was Old is not exactly a diary, neither is it a memoir. It is easier to say what it isn't than what it is, as Dr Johnson remarked of poetry; perhaps it is best described as a book of thoughts occasioned by occurrences in Simenon's daily life. The strange thing about Simenon is that he is incapable of being uninteresting, an inability that must have been innate, for no background or education could fully explain it. The opposite, alas, is by far the more common. For example, I have just spent a couple of days in the company of a visitor whose every utterance was of a mind-numbing banality. She was drawn to the obvious as a wasp to jam but could not resist expressing it. Her loquaciousness was unstoppable. She would announce that she had filled her glass with water — still, not carbonated — as if she had just returned from the far side of the moon. The worst (or second worst) of it was that she was well-meaning, which added the burden of guilt at one's exasperation to that of one's exasperation itself. In fact, she was so boring that she was almost interesting, and would have been to Simenon, whose interest in and sympathy for humanity was, at least on paper, inexhaustible.

He is not exactly a philosopher, of course, and yet his reflections are not devoid of philosophical interest:

> I am surprised at how small the number of personal ideas
> – or ideas that we believe to be personal – that we take
> with us over the years and which, sometimes, suffice to
> furnish a life.

Indeed, whole careers have been built on a single idea.

On 25 June, 1960, he wrote 'Four days ago – the 21st – I finished a novel, my hundred and eightieth plus, that I had wanted to be easy. But the first day I began to write, towards the ninth or tenth page, I had the feeling that it wasn't worth going on to the end, that I would never make anything living of it.' The book was *Maigret et les viellards* (Maigret and the Old Men), written in a week, from the 15th to the 21st June, 1960. He finished revising it on 9th July, 1960.

Though written in only a week, it has never been out of print since — and I write this precisely sixty-two years and eight days after its completion. If ever there were evidence that a Muse spoke through a human being, it is surely in the work of Simenon, prolific, amusing, but never entirely trivial.

Maigret and the Old Men begins with Maigret and his wife having one of their regular dinners with their friends, Dr and Mrs Pardon. Dr Pardon quotes an article in *The Lancet* by Dr Richard Fox (a real person who *did* write articles in *The Lancet* and whose words I now translate back into English from Dr Pardon's translation of them):

> A well-informed psychiatrist, supported by his scientific knowledge, is rather well-placed to understand men. However, it is possible, especially if he allows himself to be influenced by theory, that he understands less well than an exceptional schoolmaster, a novelist, or even a policeman.

(How right Fox was on the baleful effect of psychological theory on human understanding!)

The passage put me in mind of another in an essay by Simon Leys, the Belgian-Australian sinologist and literary essayist (Simenon was also Belgian, of course). I was very proud when Leys, in one of his books of essays, *Le bonheur des petits poissons* (The Happiness of Little Fish), quoted a column I had written in the *Spectator*, in which I had said that, other things being equal, I would rather be treated by a doctor who had read Chekhov than by one who hadn't: to which Leys added that he would rather be judged, if judged at all, by a judge who had read Simenon than by one who had not.

A passport photo taken (to judge by the style) at about the time that *Quand j'étais vieux* was published, fell out of it. The photo was of a man in tie and shirtsleeves, in his late thirties or early forties, though people aged quicker in those days so he may have been younger, with a heavy jaw and an evasive upward turn of his eyes, as if not wishing to look anyone in the face: in short, shifty. Who was he? Why did he not look straight ahead? O Maigret! O Simenon!

If someone had given me Jeanette Marks' book, *Genius and Disaster: Studies in Drugs and Genius*, blindfold to smell, I should have recognised it at once as an American book of the 1920s or 30s, for American paper of that era had a characteristic smell. This fact has, for me, all the charm of uselessness. In addition to its charm, the uselessness of a fact has the moral advantage that it cannot be used as a plank for a vicious philosophy. There is also a philosophical point to be made about the smell: if anyone were to ask me to describe it such that he would be able to recognise it himself without further assistance or information, I could not do so. This establishes the insufficiency or incompleteness of words by themselves; and indeed, if words could adequately and exhaustively describe a smell, the sense of smell itself would be redundant.

Genius and Disaster was published in 1925 and takes as its subject the relation between illness, suffering, alcohol, opium and poetry, particularly that of the English Romantics of the early nineteenth century. The author was a professor of English literature, born in 1875, who was an early feminist and lived for forty-eight years in a lesbian relationship without (so far as I know) suffering any undue social consequences. I doubt that she would have cared much for stridency, though it would now perhaps have been required of her.

Jeanette Marks wrote a book on the life and habits of insects (called, charmingly, *Little Busybodies*) and also at least two books about Wales, including *Gallant Little Wales*. I suspect, then, that she was of Welsh descent, for Marks is a name not unknown in Wales. I once interviewed the most celebrated Welshman of that name, Howard Marks, a famous or infamous smuggler of cannabis and campaigner for its legalisation, who had studied philosophy at Oxford and had written an immense best-seller recounting his life, with the title *Mr. Nice*. He was, indeed, very charming, though I sensed (without evidence, I admit) that there was an inner coldness or ruthlessness to him, of the kind that is not incompatible with social charm and affability. He was highly intelligent and quick-witted, and no sooner had I said, with regard to the so-called War on Drugs, that we should not be the prisoners of our metaphors than he said, 'That is a metaphor'. 'Touché" was all that I could reply, with real pleasure at his wit.

But to return to the other Marks who concerned herself with drugs. Her book, it seems to me, lacks a certain hard-edgedness that I would have liked, a more definite thesis to propound, being myself used to a more medical approach to the subject. Not surprisingly, Marks' approach is more biographical than numerical or epidemiological. Statistical generalisations cannot supply meanings or even satisfactory explanations of human conduct. If I were to ask why x committed suicide last year and you were to reply, 'Because the suicide rate increased by ten per cent last year during the economic downturn,' I should not reply, 'Thank you, *now* I understand.' And if you thought that you had supplied a full explanation, I should think you were a robot, not a human being; but at the same time, I would not wish to deny the explanatory value of statistics altogether. I have no way of resolving the contradiction.

The book opens with a statement that made my heart sink for a moment:

> Some one boasted to Dr Marston that he had cured a certain writer of his tendency to alcoholic overindulgence. "It is a pity," replied Dr Marston, "for he has never written a line worth reading since."

I thought, then, that the book would be a prolonged apologia for alcoholism and drug-taking as a, or even *the*, literary muse, but it is nothing of the kind. It has no clear line of argumentation, a lack that I found frustrating (I like ambiguity to arise from the world, not from the attempts of an author to describe the world), though the author does finally say that she thought that her subjects — Edgar Allan Poe, James Thomson, Algernon Swinburne and Frances Thompson — lost more than they gained from their various addictions. On the other hand, she says that the extension or slowness of the passage of time experienced by opium-takers accounts for the following verse in Thomson's most famous poem, *City of Dreadful Night*:

> The City is of Night, but not of Sleep;
>   There sweet sleep is not for the weary brain;
> The pitiless hours like years and ages creep,
>   A night seems timeless hell. The dreadful strain
> Of thought and consciousness that never ceases,
> Or which some moment's stupor but increases,
>   This worse than woe, makes wretches there insane.

This, it seems to me, is an example of what oft was thought but ne'er so well express'd: moreover, what oft was thought by those *not* under the influence of opium.

If for no other reason, Marks' book is valuable for its recognition that De Quincey's and Coleridge's principal addiction was to alcohol, not to opium, as the romantic legend would have it. They both drank formidable quantities of alcohol, Coleridge downing three bottles of claret as well as pints of laudanum (tincture of opium in alcohol) in a day. His poem, *The Pains of Sleep*, usually thought to be a poetic description of the effects of opium, strikes me as much more that of the consequences of overindulgence in alcohol. But there is no doubt that alcoholism is a lot less romantic than addiction to opium, as is bronchiectasis than tuberculosis. (No opera has ever been written, nor will ever be written, about someone dying of chronic bronchitis, a truly pitiable death.)

If Marks is very good on this question — whether alcohol or opium was the principal addiction of De Quincey and Coleridge — she is less good, in my opinion (but very good in the opinion of modern orthodoxy) on that of addiction in general. She sees it as a purely medical problem, with a few small sociological factors thrown in to a very minor extent. She says, for example, 'The use of such words as "opium sot" is a bit out of date, and is as startling to anyone intelligent about the neurosis of opium addiction as "tuberculosis soak" would be to the student of the tubercle bacillus.' In other words, addiction to opium and tuberculosis are in the same category of phenomena, namely that of illness. The author later says:

> … until the popular mind has enlarged its definition of disease to include narcomanias, as well as other types of insanity, and has stopped the time-wasting business of

condemnation, we shall look on such spectacles of disaster or the crippling of Poe, James Thomson, Swinburne, Francis Thompson, and many other poets, content to let human and spiritual waste to be a part of our civilization.

In other words, we have nothing to condemn but condemnation itself.

There is a kind of perverse logic at work here of a Pharisee nature. 'I do not sympathise with wrongdoers, but I sympathise with drug addicts, therefore drug addicts are not doing anything wrong in taking drugs. They cannot help it, poor things (unlike me, who has been lucky): they are ill. How generous-minded I am!'

There is, moreover, something incipiently totalitarian in this view, though I doubt that Marks realised it or would have approved of it had she done so:

But one who serves society rather than himself, as the man or woman of genius does, deserves at the cost of society to be shielded from those harms (himself included) to which he is particularly vulnerable.

A concentration camp for geniuses, then.

Marks suggests that Poe did not drink to excess, merely that he could not, to a pathological extent, hold his drink: in short that he suffered, though she does not use the term, from *manie à potu*, morbid intoxication, a condition in which a comparatively small quantity of alcohol has a disproportionate effect. Whether the condition actually exists or not is still a matter of dispute, but if it does (so it is said), it is more common among the brain-damaged and epileptic than among others. Turning to the third edition of William Alwyn Lishman's great book, *Organic Psychiatry: The Psychological Consequences of Cerebral Disorder*, whose first edition in 1978 I read with pleasure from cover to cover, we find the following:

> Attempts to study pathological intoxication directly have led to conflicting results. Bach-y-Rita *et al.* (1970) gave intravenous infusions of alcohol to 10 men with a history of violent outbursts when intoxicated, but in no case was the abnormal behaviour reproduced. In a similar experiment, however, Maletzky (1976) obtained the expected reactions in 15 of 22 cases. Nine became violent with inappropriate rage, four became psychotic with hallucinations and delusions, and two showed a mixture of both. The remainder developed normal intoxication only.

But Maletzky administered larger doses of alcohol, so as is usual in such research, the results were equivocal and require further research which, for ethical reasons, is unlikely ever to be done.

Professor Lishman was so accomplished a classical pianist that he considered a musical rather than a medical career. He was also the perfect gentleman. He examined my wife for a higher professional qualification and, correctly in her own estimation, failed her: but was so gentlemanly about it that it was almost a pleasure (she passed on a subsequent occasion).

217

A sentence in Marguerite Duras' *L'Amant* (The Lover) engraved itself forever on my memory, for as long as my memory lasts: *Très vite dans ma vie il a été trop tard* (Very quickly in my life it was too late). This simple sentence brings us at once to the mystery of the irreversibility of time and of all that we do in it and to that of fate itself. If it is true that one's genetic endowment plays at least a limiting if not preponderant role in determining the course of one's life, then in a sense it is already too late at the time of one's conception. Moreover, opportunities occur that will never recur: once they have gone, they have gone, and it is too late the moment that they are not seized. *Carpe diem!* — seize the day! Generally, we don't.

Duras published a novella titled *Madame Dodin* in 1954. Its protagonist, who gave to it its title, is the concierge of No. 5, rue Sainte-Eulalie in the Sixth Arrondissement of Paris, in the Latin Quarter, then still the haunt of bohemians, artists etc., among them my mother's first cousin, whom I remember as wearing a tight apple-green polo-necked sweater, deemed shocking by my father, a confirmed womaniser. She wrote a little poetry and lived for a time with Richard Wright, author of *Notes of a Native Son*, and who was disappointed when I told her that the American Hospital in Paris might not have poisoned him under the orders of the CIA, but that he might have died instead of the cardiac side-effects of emetine hydrochloride, the drug then used to treat amoebic dysentery from which Wright suffered.

Nowadays, the Sixth Arrondissement has become far too expensive to support the bohemian life, and cheaper suburbs are not propitious to it either. Bohemianism is dead.

No. 5, rue Sainte-Eulalie is on six floors, and Madame Dodin passionately hates its tenants, an *a priori* or *ex officio* passion as it were, insofar as it does not depend upon the actual behaviour of the tenants. Rather, it is a matter of principle with her: why should they get to lead their lives while she is only their concierge? Her strongest ostensible complaint is in the matter of their dustbins: they do not empty them every day into the collective dustbin as she thinks that they should and as she herself does. The novella begins:

> Every morning, Mme Dodin, our concierge, takes out her dustbin. She drags it from the little inner courtyard of the building out on to the street – with all her strength, without care, on the contrary – in the hope of making us jump in our beds, and that our slumbers will be interrupted, as are hers, every morning.

When she pulls her dustbin over the two steps from the entrance of No. 5 on to the street, 'a kind of clatter results which she hopes will wake us up.'

This took me straight back to the hospital in which I worked for many years. My office gave out by means of frosted windows on to a narrow outside passageway open to the sky between two buildings. I could see nothing through the windows, but every morning, at about eleven in the morning, a kind of vehicle would go by with a noise similar to that made by a theatrical thunder-making machine. As it approached my window, passed it and continued on its way, all conversation, indeed all thought, had to be held in abeyance.

One day I decided to go out and see what this formidable

vehicle was. I was expecting a juggernaut of some description. I discovered to my surprise that, just as some very small men surprise by their *basso profundo* voices, the formidable vehicle was actually composed of three small wire cages on little castor wheels. The cages were used for collecting and distributing laundry in the hospital, on this occasion only a handful of sheets and pillowcases. I couldn't help laughing, but actually there was something more serious behind the absurdity.

The thunder-making contraption was pushed all round the hospital. If I had not known better, I should have said that years of research had gone into producing a vehicle with so high a noise to load ratio. The fact is that nobody in the hospital administration, by no means a negligible proportion of the hospital's overall staff, had noticed the noise or given it any thought. That it was horrible, disturbing to patients and quite unnecessary did not occur to them or, if it did, appear to them of any importance. The fact that it was so easily remediable would have deterred them also, for administrations like difficulty or impossibility rather than ease of solution to problems, for difficulty and impossibility are felt by them to be guarantees of continuous employment. Besides, patients were felt to be lucky to get what they were given and tended in any case by their very nature to get in the way of the smooth running of the organisation. When I wrote to the chief executive of the hospital, he did not reply, and nothing was done. I was more of a nuisance than the thunder-making machine.

I began even to wonder whether the administrators actually approved of this vehicle as some kind of revenge to be wrought upon patients for making the running of the hospital so complicated. If only they could be driven away. In *Madame Dodin* there is an interesting and amusing passage about her inner motivation, why she so hates the tenants of the building, and why she wants to make them suffer. There is a timid neighbour of No. 5, an old spinster called Mlle Mimi, who for six years has provided Mme Dodin, free of charge, with delicious meals. But this does not alter or soften Mme Dodin's view of the world and humanity:

> Her repulsion at human egoism was not softened [by Mlle Mimi's generosity]. For nothing, apart possibly the suppression of the institution of the dustbin, nothing would ever begin to reduce Mme Dodin's dissatisfaction. She had grasped once and for all, in a lightning flash of illumination, the scope of universal injustice. Since then, none of the individual cases of happiness or goodness that she had encountered shook or reduced her scepticism. Mme Dodin was perfectly impervious to charity.

We have all known people like this, whose rage against the world nothing can assuage. And yet such people are not necessarily altogether unhappy, for there is in their resentment a sour satisfaction — and self-satisfaction. No one would be more disappointed that Mme Dodin if all her complaints about dustbins were resolved: not, of course, that there is the slightest chance of this, for the production of waste is an inevitable consequence of our way of life, and it has to be disposed of somehow. Mme Dodin can resent the vegetable peelings of the tenants as long as she is a concierge, and complaint is her only joy.

There is something else about Mme Dodin that is frequently the case with such people: she inspires fear in such a way that no one opposes her. She is ignorant, charmless, not particularly intelligent, and yet the tenants, better in every way, are afraid to confront her though in fact she has no real power over them. They submit to her ill-temper and her minor acts of despotism without protest. I have seen this many times in institutions: the narrow-minded, the stupid, the transparently mediocre are able to attain and retain power because, like the tenants of No. 5, rue Sainte-Eulalie, they avoid confrontation, so that idiocy goes by default.

One last word: in taking a concierge as her protagonist (there is a sub-protagonist, Gaston, who is a street sweeper), she renders a human service. How easy it is to disregard entirely the lives of those who serve us, to make of them but animated furniture, with no lives, thoughts or feelings of their own. By *us* I mean the consumers of services, the bourgeois bohemians with thoughts on higher things than the emptying of dustbins.

When I was a boy, Albert Schweitzer was one of the most famous people in the world, physically resembling Einstein somewhat, and was regarded nearly as a saint. He had abandoned everything — a brilliant career as a musicologist, organist and theologian — to bury himself in darkest Africa, in order to bring succour to the poor Africans. Could selflessness go further?

But in the modern world, if a hero comes, can debunking be far behind? The biography of few people is incapable of being written as the case for the prosecution for an adolescent or young adult mind, as nothing but a chronicle of hypocrisy, dishonesty, peccadilloes, etc. At the tender age of fifteen, I read Gerald McKnight's damning polemical study, against rather than of Schweitzer. Far from having been self-abnegating, Schweitzer was a publicity-seeking authoritarian egotist, a kind of Alsatian Mrs Jellyby, who sacrificed his wife and daughter to himself on the altar of his fame. His hospital at Lambaréné was a disorganised and unhygienic shambles that did little good if any. The *New York Times* in its review thought the book so intemperate and relentless that it concluded that McKnight must nevertheless have thought that there was a fund of greatness in Schweitzer for him to be worth attacking in this way. I am not sure that this is correct: that is to say, that there are no idols worthy to be destroyed in this way. But was Schweitzer an idol who was undeservedly and incontinently worshipped? I rather doubt it, thought certainly the passage of time has eroded him to the point of invisibility. I have not done the experiment, but I suspect that if I were to show a picture of him to people under the age of fifty, very few, even among the highly educated, would recognise him.

No reasonable person could deny that Schweitzer was a very considerable person. He was a Bach scholar of the first rank, and I am told by people who know about such things that his huge book on Bach was the greatest work ever devoted to that composer. He was also a theologian of some standing, though here again I am not competent to judge. He was neither a complete pacifist nor a vegetarian, but he tended in those directions, and certainly he was against nuclear war, signing declarations in favour of the abolition of nuclear weapons. But what use were these declarations? There is, to my mind, a soapy quality about them that makes one wish almost to oppose them, though no one longs for nuclear war.

One of the accusations against Schweitzer was that he was condescending towards Africans, that he did not treat them as equals, and did not even think of them as such. He said that they were his brothers, but his younger brothers. When the British journalist, James Cameron, visited Lambaréné in 1953, he found the hospital not only disorganised but Schweitzer's attitude towards the Africans degrading. He suppressed his criticisms, however, for 1953 was not yet an era of iconoclasm. McKnight's book was published eleven years later. The intellectual and social atmosphere had changed.

Certainly, in a book like *More from the Primeval Forest*, published in 1931 as a sequel to *From the Primeval Forest* published in 1924, one can find material for the case for the prosecution. Schweitzer calls the Africans from deeper into the interior than Lambaréné 'savages', which no one would dare do now. His characterisation of the 'savages' is not flattering. It is startling to read the following written by the great humanitarian: 'The midday hour is the worst of the whole day, for then every creature that can crawl comes to the consulting room and asks for a "ration".' Schweitzer finds them childish and exasperating, incapable of providence or logical reflection. 'These savages are very susceptible to the damp atmosphere of the forest. Then why do they not spend part of their wages on mosquito nets and blankets? Because mosquito nets are expensive, and being real savages they would rather buy tobacco and trifles than useful things.'

To this day, the well-placed (including me) are irritated by the tendency of the poor — in western societies, the relatively poor — to fritter away on gewgaws whatever disposable income they may have that are worth nothing the moment they buy them and cease to please almost immediately afterwards. The extension of credit to the poor has encouraged them to indebt themselves for the sake of what amount to toys: they have long lost all peasant shrewdness and seem to have become children again with little self-control, unable to postpone gratification and prey to desire for any novelty. As to honouring their debts, it is a matter of what they are forced to do: there is no dishonour in dishonouring them (as there once was). The riposte of the poor would be, 'Try being poor yourself before criticising us.' George Orwell wrote about the propensity of the poor of his day — and *they* were poor in a more absolute sense than the poor today — to buy food that was 'tasty' rather than nutritious according to the dietary doctrines of the day.

Schweitzer continues, '"Then their masters should be obliged to provide them with mosquito nets and blankets!" Quite right, But they would soon barter the blankets and nets for bananas or baubles of any sort which were offered them by a native from the neighbourhood, just as they dispose of their masters' axes and bush knives for a trifle, and then declare that they are lost.'

One group, the Bendjabis, excites his particular frustration or disdain. 'Being real savages, they are a painful distance "beyond good and evil."[34] The rules which govern life for the

---

[34] Surely a dig at Nietzsche.

hospital inmates are to them mere words which do not concern them… This unsuccessful struggle, repeated day after day, to produce in these savages some notion of what is meant by value, is a trial of patience and nerves as severe as that anyone could imagine.'

The interaction of two different conceptions of life is rich with possible misunderstandings.

As is so often the case, passages in obscure books (and though best-sellers in their time, I think it safe to say that Schweitzer's books about the primeval forest have now entered obscurity) are like the madeleine in Proust. Schweitzer wrote:

> Sometimes I have to deal with natives who were in Europe as soldiers during the war [the First World War, of course]. The one with whom I get on best is a Pahouin who never boasts of any heroic deeds… Through questions that I put to the man about the gold crowns on some of his teeth, I learnt that my patient had been in Europe and in military service, though he had said nothing about it. These crowns did not imply any damage to the teeth, but the black soldiers made a practice of getting them put on to make an impression on their people at home.

In my years in medical practice in one of the poorest parts of a large British city, and in a prison, I had as patients a number of young men whose front teeth glistened with gold. Some had even had gold stars inlaid as dental marquetry in their incisors. None of this golden dentistry was necessitated by disease of their teeth. It was, rather, a sign of their success and perhaps of their dangerousness — for they were all drug-dealers. We still live in the primeval forest.

There are a number of photographs in Schweitzer's book, some of them of groups of Africans. What is striking to me about them (as in other books of the time about Africa) is how miserable they all look. When I travelled through Africa more than half a century later, crossing the continent by public transport, such as it was, I did not encounter such miserable faces, though they may have returned in the thirty-five years since my journey.

But the most startling photograph of all is that of Schweitzer himself that is the frontispiece, which shows him in profile, dressed in white ducks, sitting on the ground with a large river and palm trees and other tropical vegetation in the background. Were it not for this, I could have sworn it was Joseph Stalin sitting there.

A Russian friend of mine — or at least a friend of mine who spent the first twenty-five years of his life in Russia but who would not now care to call himself a Russian — maintains that no one in the West, or at any rate vanishingly few, understands Russia. Whether the West in his estimation includes Bulgaria and Romania, say, I am not quite certain, but he sets up an antinomy which is almost a cliché — which is not to say that it is false.

To deceive the West has long been the aim of Russians, both of their governments and themselves. In his book, *Russia in 1839*, the Marquis de Custine, who went to Russia in search of arguments in favour of autocratic monarchy, his relatives having been guillotined in the Revolution, and returned a democrat, says that he did not blame the Russians for being what they were but for pretending to be what they were not. Different as the mentalities of the English, the French and the Germans may have been, the differences between them were minor compared with their differences from the Russians.

As a Pole who had gone as a boy into exile in Russia with his father, Joseph Conrad could hardly be accused of naivety about, ignorance of or excessive love for the Russians. His novel *Under Western Eyes*, published in 1911 in the wake of the first and failed Russian Revolution, is clearly of the school that suggests that the Russians are of a completely different mentality from westerners, the latter of whom do not at all understand the former.

The story takes place between St Petersburg and Geneva. The protagonist, Razumov, is a student at the university who is not one of the revolutionary intellectuals (virtually a pleonasm at the time). One day a revolutionary student called Haldin, without asking his permission or even knowing his true opinions, which include belief in the Tsarist autocracy, takes refuge in his rooms on the day on which he has assassinated a cruel Tsarist functionary. Razumov betrays Haldin to the authorities and he is hanged, but the revolutionaries do not know of Razumov's betrayal and regard him as an associate of Haldin's 'heroic' act. (The assassination is reminiscent of that of Alexander II, the Tsar Liberator, who, driving through Petersburg in his coach, survived the first bomb of an assassination attempt, only to be killed by a second bomb while he was trying to succour the injured victims of the first. What head of state today would behave, or would be allowed to behave, in this way? Napoleon III, though he survived, behaved similarly. What does this difference tell us, if anything?)

Because Razumov is believed by the revolutionaries to be one of their own, he is sent by the Tsarist secret service to Geneva to spy on the revolutionists who have taken refuge there, under the pretext that he is about to be arrested himself as an associate of Haldin's. There he meets Haldin's sister with whom he falls in love. Overcome by remorse, he confesses his treachery to a roomful of revolutionaries, one of whom, Nikita, is a ferocious, pitiless and brutal murderer of policemen and gendarmes. This Nikita attacks Razumov, bursting both his eardrums by terrific blows on the side of the head (Nikita takes pride in knowing how to do it), as a result of which Razumov is instantly rendered deaf. Because of his deafness, he is soon run over by a tram whose approach he does not hear (rather like an electric car today) and is crippled for life. In a final twist, Nikita is revealed as a Tsarist agent himself, who kills policemen and gendarmes in order to gain the trust of the inner circle of revolutionaries, the better to betray them. One could hardly capture the contortions of the revolution and the counterrevolution better than in this novel — which was not altogether a success in England when first published, perhaps because the smug English novel-reading public of the time found it hard to credit such twisted mentalities.

Razumov remains a very Russian type, the kind who looks on Western prosperity with contempt, regarding it not as a triumph of human ingenuity and organisation but as a symptom of spiritual deadness, a trope that Mr Putin still employs today — as does Miss Haldin of the novel. Her conservative and revolutionary selves are at one in this. Of her, the narrator says, 'That propensity of lifting every problem from the plane of the understandable by means of some sort of mystic expression, is very Russian. I know her [Miss Haldin] well enough to discover her scorn for all practical forms of political liberty known to the western world.' According to reports, the mind of Vladimir Putin is full of mystico-philosophico-geopolitico rubbish, combined with the morality of the black mamba.

Razumov looks on the scene of the shores of Lake Geneva and thinks it odious — oppressively odious — in its unsuggestive finish: 'the very perfection of mediocrity attained at last after centuries of toil and culture.' Who, reading this, is not reminded of Harry Lime's famous remark in *The Third Man* about the five hundred years of democracy giving birth to the cuckoo clock? A little later in *Under Western Eyes*, the narrator, supposedly an English teacher of languages in Geneva, writes, 'now and then, after the faint flash, there was a faint sleepy rumble; but the main forces of the thunderstorm remained Massed down the Rhone valley as if loath to attack the respectable and passionless abode of democratic liberty, the serious-minded town of dreary hotels, tendering the same indifferent hospitality to tourists of all nations and to international conspirators of every shade.'

It is difficult to believe that Conrad himself did not share this view, though it is often an elementary critical error to identify an author's views with those of his narrator. In any case, I confess that on my own visits to Geneva, a century later, I shared the narrator's views. Staying in ordinary Swiss hotels, which are better than French ones (let alone British), I almost immediately felt a kind of suffocation and before long was seeking out that part of town that was the abode of African refugees of many types, eating in their restaurants and talking to them. I doubt that they were revolutionists, though some of them might have been dreamers, but at any rate I found them more attractive, humanly, than the correct citizens of the city.

'I think you people are under a curse,' says the narrator of the Russians, and again it is difficult not to believe this is Conrad's view also. Indeed, it is difficult not to believe that he was right, considering the history of Russia after he wrote. He says of Haldin's mother, exiled in Geneva, that 'she was under the evil spell of an arbitrary rule: a victim of tyranny and revolution…'

If anything, Conrad hates the latter more than the former. He despises 'the invincible belief in the advent of loving concord springing like a heavenly flower from the soil of men's earth, torn by struggles, watered with tears.' Through his narrator, he speaks prophetically:

> … in a real revolution, the best characters do not come to the fore. A violent revolution falls into the hands of narrow-minded fanatics and of tyrannical hypocrites at first. Afterward comes the turn of the pretentious intellectual failures of the time. Such are the chiefs and the leaders. You will notice that I have left out the mere rogues. The scrupulous and the just, the noble, humane and devoted natures; the unselfish and the intelligent may begin a movement – but it passes away from them. They

are not the leaders of a revolution. They are its victims: the victims of disgust, of disenchantment – often of remorse. Hopes grotesquely betrayed, ideal caricatured – that is the definition of revolutionary success.

Of course, Conrad was understating the case.

In his book, *Dora Bruder*, Patrick Modiano writes that 'Number 39 [boulevard Ornano] has an inscription indicating the name of its architect, a certain Pierrefeu, and the date of its construction, 1881. The same was almost certainly true of Number 41.' The latter was the address where Dora Bruder had lived.

These little inscriptions indicating the names of the architect are common in Paris of the post-Franco-Prussian War. They are fitting memorials to architects who thought that it was their duty to produce buildings that harmonised and gave rise to a civilised and cultivated urban way of life. Although their buildings were not exactly alike, yet they did nothing to make them stand out to assault the eye like a splinter. Thus no one could look at Number 41, boulevard Ornano and say to himself, 'Obviously the work of Pierrefeu.' I contrast this laudable modesty with the raving, psychopathic, narcissistic egotism of, say, Frank Gehry's atrocious tower in Arles, a textbook example of how to ruin an immemorial townscape with a single prepotent building which it is impossible to exclude from one's view. It screams Frank Gehry! Frank Gehry! Frank Gehry! Frank Gehry! Frank Gehry! Frank Gehry! and will do so long as it stands.

Naturally, it cost far too much to build for anyone to demolish it, demolition being the only hope of improvement.

But to be fair to Frank Gehry, which does not come naturally to me, he could not have destroyed the townscape alone. He needed an equally egotistical patron and a supine, possibly corrupt, city council to commission and permit such a building. No doubt they were terrorised intellectually by the fear of being accused of not 'understanding' Gehry's design and of being reactionary if they sought something that would merely harmonise with the city. The one thing that can be said for the Luma Tower, I suppose, is that it saved on the need for an inscription to inform the public 'Frank Gehry *architecte*': a trifling saving, though, to set against the financial, aesthetic and moral cost.

Modiano's novel was published in 1997 and consists of the attempt by the narrator to reconstruct the trajectory and short life of Dora Bruder, in whom he becomes interested when he sees a small ad enquiring after her whereabouts while leafing through the newspaper, *Paris Soir*, for 1941. (After the Liberation in 1944, the newspaper was considered to have been collaborationist and was closed down.) Of course, even to be leafing through the newspaper for 1941 implies a certain pre-existing interest in those times, which many people might not share, either from indifference or from a guilt or uneasiness about them, even if they could not be held personally responsible for anything that happened during them.

Modiano had, in fact, a special reason to interest himself in that epoch. He was born very shortly after the end of the war in Europe; his father, of Italian-Jewish descent survived the

Occupation by expedients that were, perhaps, as morally ambiguous as those of, say, George Soros under the Nazis and Communists in Budapest. He was even rumoured to have been a collaborator in Paris with the French arm of the Gestapo. I think this is enough to explain Modiano's relationship with the not very distant past, very fruitful from the literary point of view.

Dora Bruder was the daughter of Austrian and Hungarian Jewish parents who migrated to France in the wake of the First World War. They were poor and lived for years in a single hotel room at 41, boulevard Ornano. For safety, Dora was sent to a Catholic boarding school from which, however, she ran away. In the meantime, her father was arrested and sent to the camp at Drancy, from which, like his daughter, he was sent to Auschwitz to be murdered. He was 43, she 16. His wife, her mother, was sent to Auschwitz five months later. Modiano tries to reconstruct Dora's life from the exiguous documentation that remains and intertwines it with his equally exiguous knowledge of his own father's life.

Is it morbid to dwell so on events of more than half a century ago? The Occupation was part of the French past that, in Henry Rousso's famous phrase, does not pass: or certainly had not passed by 1996, when Modiano wrote the book.

For example, my mother-in-law, a Parisian who was exactly Dora Bruder's age when she lived through the Occupation, had vivid memories of it. At the beginning of the Occupation, she kept a square of chocolate (then a greater luxury than any luxury today), promising herself that she would eat it only when she won the Latin prize at school. When she did win it, however, the chocolate had deteriorated so that it was inedible. A small thing, of course, and not a great tragedy by the standards of the time, but still unimaginable to a young person of today. How could anybody be so fixated on so meagre a pleasure as a square of chocolate?

Many years later, some time in the early 2000s, my mother-in-law was on a bus in Paris when she fell to talking to a lady of her own age who was sitting next to her. Her interlocutor asked her where she lived. 'Avenue Gambetta,' she replied. What number? What floor? (One does not have to hide things from ladies in their 80s.) When told, her interlocutor burst into tears. My mother-in-law's flat was where she, Jewish, spent the entire Occupation, hiding from the authorities. She could not even approach the window, for opposite was the *Kommandantur*, the local headquarters of the occupying forces (before and afterwards a police station). For years, then, she had lived in a state of terror — helpless and confined terror — in the very rooms of my mother-in-law's flat, the supposedly best years of her life. How can such a past pass so long as there is anyone alive to remember it? One would not have dared to ask her the fate of her parents: a Dora Bruder mystery.

Two flights up from my mother-in-law's flat lived a lady three years younger than she, whose older brother was rounded up in the last such round-up before the end of the Occupation and deported to Estonia, from which he never returned (of all the several hundred in that convoy of deportees, only twenty returned). Shortly before Modiano's book was published, my mother-in-law's neighbour placed an advertisement in a newspaper to ask whether there were any surviving relatives of the deported in that convoy and, receiving many replies, she founded an association of relatives and survivors, for which work she later received the *Légion d'honneur*; my wife and I attended the conferral ceremony that was held at the *Mémorial de la Shoah* (one of the few museums in the world permanently guarded by men with automatic weapons). It was given her, on behalf of the President, by the French ambassador to Estonia.

Modiano tells us that many of the haunts of Dora Bruder were demolished after the war and replaced by concrete buildings 'the colour of amnesia'. This is a fine image. Even where it is not the colour of amnesia, it is the colour of depersonalisation in the psychiatric sense.[35]

Towards the end of the book, Modiano refers to a list of the four thousand children who arrived in Dora's camp for deportation to Auschwitz. 'The names of many of them had been hastily written on their clothes [but] they were now unreadable. Child without identity No. 122. Child without identity No. 146. Little girl aged three. First name Monique. Without identity.'

By strange coincidence, my copy of the book bore the following inscription in a cultivated hand: Monique R, May, 1997.

This is the kind of coincidence that would have set Modiano's imagination racing. It was extremely unlikely to be the same Monique, of course. Not only was the writing not of someone of that era (albeit that this is not firm evidence), but any three-year-old Monique transported to Auschwitz could

---

[35] Depersonalisation is the feeling of disconnection from one's body and thoughts, a symptom often of anxiety.

not have survived. But why did Monique R. dispose of the book? It was slim enough not to have cluttered even a cluttered home, and people who buy relatively expensive first editions as they are published do not usually dispose of books lightly, certainly not after having inscribed them with their names. Perhaps Monique R. died and her legatees wanted to disembarrass themselves of her belongings. Or perhaps the coincidence of names evoked such terrible associations that she decided to rid herself of the book after all, not so that she could rid herself of those associations, but at least put them to the back of her mind.

Who knows? Who can ever know?

Brendan Lehane's book, *The Compleat Flea* (presumably a reference to Walton's *The Compleat Angler*) begins with a charming first line of acknowledgments: 'I am very grateful to Mr F.G.A.M. Smit, Custodian of the Flea Department at Tring…' This reads as if everyone were familiar with the Flea Department at Tring, or aware of its existence, which I suspect is not the case. Certainly, it was not so in *my* case, though now I intend one day to familiarise myself with it.

The book was published in 1969. Franciscus Gerardus Albertus Maria Smit (1920 – 2000) was a Dutch-born entomologist who moved to England to be custodian of the flea and lice collection at Tring founded by Charles, brother of the second Lord Rothschild, and now part of the British Museum (Natural History). Charles Rothschild discovered and described 500 species of flea, and the collection, the largest in the world, has 250,000 specimens. His brother built the museum at Tring. Lord Rothschild's niece, Miriam, also became the world's greatest expert on fleas, who (among many other achievements) elucidated the mechanism of the flea's powerful jump, and her son became an eminent biologist. In addition to being a banking dynasty, then, the Rothschilds became a biological dynasty, in the sense of biology as a science. Miriam's father, paternal uncle, brother and son were all biologists of the highest calibre. This is interesting in itself, for it suggests that great inherited wealth is not by itself a cause of degeneracy, as popular prejudice would have it.

My own connection with fleas has been slight, I am glad to say. I have not studied them closely, though on one occasion they studied me closely. (I return to the stories of my infestation by arthropods.) It was in East Africa where I suffered from jiggers, the flea of the species *Tunga penetrans*. The appalling female of this creature burrows into the soft tissue between one's toes and grows into a petit pois-sized swelling, having mated with the male from the vantage point of her new home. (Imagine the patient study necessary to establish this fact, a trillionth of all that Mankind has learned about the natural world!) Colonisation of the foot by the flea can lead to gangrene, the loss of toes and death: Albert Schweitzer said that he rarely saw a patient with all ten toes. The only case of *tetanic opisthotonos* that I ever saw was in East Africa, of a patient whose jiggers had been the point of entry into his body of the tetanus germ.[36] He died.

---

[36] Opisthotonos is a condition in which the muscles of the neck, back and legs contract and lead to a stiff arching of the torso.

My own jiggers were less severe, which is to say less numerous. I was shown how to remove them with a pin. They had to be removed whole, for if one broke them in the process of removal, they died and the foot festered. I forgot my moral outrage at being parasitised by a lower creature of no intelligence in the intriguing and satisfying task of removing it, which required intense and undistracted concentration, in which all other worries disappeared. It was gratifying to see the smooth and painless, almost elegant, crater left behind in one's flesh. It taught me to regard this part of my anatomy dispassionately, with disinterested curiosity. The ability to detach oneself from oneself is very important in life and very helpful in difficult situations. Once, when I was being mildly assaulted with a truncheon by an Albanian policeman, what I was thinking was 'How am I going to describe this?' rather than 'Ouch!' or 'How dare he infringe my human rights as a very important person!' I used to tell my patients that it was far more important for them to be able to lose themselves than find themselves (whatever the latter might mean). I do not think, however, that many believed me, or if they believed me were able in practice to follow my advice. How, they asked, does one learn to lose oneself? Perhaps *Tunga penetrans* was put on this earth to teach us.

Brendan Lehane (1936 – 2020) was not an entomologist. He was inspired to write about fleas by a stay in Dublin in the 1960s, when he rented a cheap flat infested with fleas. How times have changed in half a century! You couldn't find a flea in Dublin now, let alone a cheap flat. The normal human flea, *Pulex irritans*, that has accompanied man throughout civilisation, is in the process of disappearing altogether from

239

our lives. When one looks at the elegant portraits of the past, one forgets that all those elegantly-clad people were plagued by fleas which they regarded, no doubt, as coterminous with human existence itself. It is easy to deny progress; but when we consider how little we are now bothered with or by arthropod parasites, as well as by nematodes and cestodes, deny the fact of progress who may!

The Compleat Flea reminded me, naturally, of my own parasitism by arthropods other than the sandflea (*Tunga penetrans*). First was by the tumbu fly, *Cordolybia anthropophaga*, which is what is called an obligate parasite, which is to say a creature that cannot live without its parasitism (one author cited by Lehane included investment bankers in this class). The tumbu fly lays its eggs on the ground, on which clothes may be laid to dry and on which the larvae emerge. I quote from the nineteenth edition (1987) of *Manson's Tropical Diseases*, page 1463:

> On hatching the minute larvae... hold themselves erect, while waving the anterior part in search of a host and can remain alive without food for about 9 days. The larvae are sensitive to both heat and vibration and once they become attached to a host immediately begin to penetrate the unbroken skin, taking approximately one minute. Penetration is usually painless...

The larvae develop into pupae, which then grow in the subcutaneous tissue. They breathe through a spiracle that emerges from the swelling that they cause, which gives Man his opportunity to disembarrass himself of these horrible maggots (everyone hates a maggot), by covering the spiracle with petroleum jelly. Unable to breathe, the maggots emerge with their hands up like gangsters surrounded by cops. I observed this on myself, again with a certain fascinated detachment, though of course aesthetically appalled.

My third infestation was with the scabies mite, *Sarcoptes scabei*. I was infested when I treated a patient in the South Seas who had Norwegian scabies, a generalised scabies over the whole surface of the body rather than the more common form which occurs between the webbing of the fingers (which is what I contracted). Norwegian scabies, so-called, is highly contagious because of the huge numbers of mites in the skin. Suffice it to say that the mite is not an attractive creature, either in its effects or visually under the microscope, though one might admire the intricacy of its form.

My fourth infestation by arthropod was in France, when I laid down in the field in front of my house to read and sleep. I was penetrated by a single tick, probably *Ixodes ricinus*. Ticks, says Manson, 'are bigger versions of mites and lack the prominent hairs found on mites.' Originally, they were parasites of reptiles but jumped taxonomic orders as countries change alliances and attached themselves to mammals — such as men. My tick grew in size as it sucked my blood, having started as a tiny black spit on the inside of my leg. I dug it out but, afraid of contracting Lyme disease that such ticks can spread, I contacted an expert on infectious diseases to ask him whether I should take antibiotics prophylactically. No, not necessary, he said; await developments. I took the antibiotics. I am a typical patient.

What I was afraid of was of falling ill and a doctor refusing to listen to my tale of tick-bite.

One of the most intriguing passages in Lehane's book is the following:

> Karl von Frisch, a popular German entomologist [who discovered the language of the dance of the bees] once shared a hotel room with a friend in Naples. The two men were attending a conference in the town. Fleas infested the room, and each evening before going to bed both scholars paraded in nightgown ritual up and down the room, attracting latent fleas. Then they swiftly stripped, caught and counted. Von Frisch's average was a bag of five, his friend' thirty or forty. The friend was obviously more magnetic. Nevertheless, it was Frisch who suffered most. Each of his bites became a large red blister. His friend's could hardly be seen.

This was a partial — a very partial — answer to something that had long puzzled me, though with an idle and lazy puzzlement. When I was a boy, I noticed that mosquitoes were attracted to my brother but not to me, just as in the case above cited, though unlike Frisch's friend, he was also much bothered by their bites. I have observed a similar difference with my wife. One day I will check the scientific literature on this. In the meantime, should I be offended that mosquitoes do not find me attractive?

Another question: before there were men, what did the human flea (or the flea of humans), *Pulex irritans*, do for a living? Or did it evolve with man himself?

My handsome book, *Insects and Other Arthropods of Medical*

Importance, edited by Kenneth G. V. Smith, published in 1973 by the British Museum (Natural History) does not address itself to this intriguing question, though it has the most interesting snippets in the midst of its rather dry text, such as 'the bites of *Scolopendra subspinipes* [a centipede] were never fatal to guinea pigs' and 'A number of cases of pseudoparasitism by centipedes have been reported', among them 'a case of intestinal pseudoparasitism lasting nine hours in Split, Yugoslavia, where a 55-year-old woman accidentally swallowed a chilopod, subsequently determined as *Scolopendra cingulata*.' The symptoms were 'vomiting, cold perspiration, irregular heart beat and sudden discharge from the bowels.'

It cannot be easy to swallow a centipede whole, which I suppose is why there are not many case reports.

Mistrusting somewhat H.G. Wells' characterisation of his mistress of ten years, Odette Keun, as a mythomaniac hysteric (he even turned the occasion on which he hit her, which he admitted in the third volume of his autobiography, against her, as evidence of how provocative she could be), and not recognising his own tendency to caddishness or acting the bounder, I decided to read what Wells called her best book, *Sous Lénine: Notes d'une femme déportée en Russie par les Anglais* (Under Lenin: notes of a Woman Deported to Russia by the English). It was published in Paris in 1922, the year following the events described in it.

In 1921, but not for much longer, the British were in control of Constantinople. Keun was a journalist who arrived there after a journey in the Caucasus. She was a socialist, indeed a communist, at the time, who openly proclaimed her sympathies in her newspaper articles. The British authorities, making no distinction between a theoretical sympathiser and an active revolutionary, summarily deported her on a boat for the Crimea. She has very harsh things to say not only about the British army, but about the British character — though perhaps strangely, she chose to settle in Britain for the second half of her life, dying on the south coast in 1978 at the age of 90. How I wish I could have known her!

Her deportation by dim, inflexible and heartless authorities reminded me of a similar episode in my own life, the only time I have been deported from a country. I arrived in Honduras from El Salvador in the pick-up truck I had bought to drive around Central America in. I had bought a lot of books in *La Catedral de libros* (the Cathedral of Books), the largest bookstore in San Salvador at the time, where I found the *Communist Manifesto* displayed on the same table as *Cafeomancia*, the art of telling the future by means of coffee grounds left in the cup: an appropriate juxtaposition when you come to think of it. The Honduran customs and immigration thought that the possession of so many books was suspect and concluded that I must be a political activist, of course of far-left tendencies, so they insisted that I left the country at once in the direction of Nicaragua, then a left-wing despotism rather than just a despotism. They provided me with a soldier to accompany me to the border, who mounted into the cab, his gun on his lap pointing in my direction. So dangerous did he consider me that he fell asleep at once. I could easily have overpowered him but instead bought him lunch when we stopped. He was, I imagine, a poor recruit; it is a strange thing to feel sorry for the person deporting you.

A further irony awaited. I had taken with me as a hitch-hiker (he rode in the back to make room for the soldier) a young Mexican who was a true believer in the Sandinista Revolution, and who had with him a large quantity of revolutionary literature, but when we arrived at the Nicaraguan border, the Nicaraguan authorities would not allow him entry because he did not have the requisite $60 with him. Thus, an anti-revolutionary was deported from an anti-revolutionary country, and a revolutionary was not allowed to enter a revolutionary one, thanks to respective officialdom. And if there is irony in small things, may there not be irony in large?

Keun is very hard on the British but, though she is a self-proclaimed sympathiser with communism (in the abstract, it is perfectly obvious that she is a thoroughgoing bourgeois), she is very much harder on the Bolsheviks. She was with them for three months, in Crimea, Ukraine and Moscow, and the value of her book is the immediacy of its testimony, its absence of hindsight. And what she saw with great clarity, only four years after the revolution, was the deformation of the human soul wrought by the Bolsheviks, which she did not excuse or attenuate by reference to the appalling conditions of the time — for which they themselves were largely responsible.

She understood that the terror created by the Cheka, the Extraordinary Commission for the Repression of Counter-revolutionary Crimes, Speculation and Abuses by High Functionaries, was not a passing phase, but an essential feature, in fact the *sine qua non*, of Bolshevik rule:

The Cheka insinuates itself into the subtlest domain of life. It exercises surveillance over politics, business, finance, family and social relations – and over thought. Thanks to it, the individual does not have the right to possess his soul. It emits vibrations and effluvia which bathe and penetrate everything, and which are of a sovereign malignity. One cannot escape the control of its agents... and since everything falls under its purview, and one can exist only by disobeying the laws, it has only an embarrassment of riches in choosing how to destroy someone when it wants to.

This and other things never changed, or change. Keun says:

It is certain that the natural resources of Russia are fabulous. But first the foreign capitalists, in order to exploit the limitless lands, would need so much money that they would have to form consortia, not only companies; second, the guarantees that the Russian government offers are so arbitrary that all enterprises of this type would be undergoing a real adventure and, to compensate for the risks, would require prodigious profits. Furthermore, the Bolsheviks are not encouraging: they assert, almost right in the faces of those talking to them, that their promises have no intrinsic value, that all ruses are permitted that achieve their end, and that in spite of any treaties, they will retake their lands as soon as the capitalists have rendered them profitable.

Interestingly, Keun was in the Soviet Union for only three

months, as the Marquis de Custine had been in Russia nearly a century earlier: insight is not proportional to length of stay, therefore. (It remained an imprisonable offence to read Custine under the Soviets, let alone disseminate it.) Both Keun and Custine changed their ideas under the influence of experience.

Keun describes the attitude of the Bolsheviks to art and literature at the time of Proletkult. She quotes an official document:

> The proletariat must filter these works [the art of pre-Revolutionary eras] through its own critique, according to its own interpretation. Then only the works that serve as a powerful weapon, in its struggle against the *ancien régime*, will constitute for it a precious heritage. It is proletarian criticism that has the task of making clear the meaning of this heritage.

When reading this, who cannot think of the present mania for reading, looking at and criticising all the works or achievements of the past through the lens of current preoccupations, racism, sexism, misogyny, etc., adopting the form, if not entirely the content, of Soviet-style criticism? Who really won the Cold War?

Titles of dry academic works or official reports can intrigue, and years ago (I forget when) I bought a copy of *Basutoland Medicine Murder: A Report on the Current Outbreak of "Diretlo" Murders in Basutoland*, published in 1951 in the traditional blue covers of British official reports. It was written by Gwilliam Iwan Jones (1904 – 1995), as his name suggests a Welshman, a colonial official turned academic social anthropologist, an expert on the art of Eastern Nigeria. Who could, or would, not be intrigued by the title of his report?

I must have bought the book not very long after my one and only visit to Basutoland, which was by then Lesotho. This small landlocked country is entirely surrounded by South Africa and was preserved from the worst psychological effects of apartheid by the fact that it had been annexed by Great Britain and administered directly as a colony rather than through the Union, then Republic, of South Africa. As this report tells us with magnificent demographic pseudoaccuracy, the population of Basutoland increased from 127,707 in 1875 to 559,273 in 1936; and the land for agriculture having become overcrowded and eroded, it acted as a labour reserve for the mines and factories of South Africa, which it remains to this day despite its formal political independence.

I remember little of my visit except that all the policemen in Maseru, the capital, seemed to be drunk, though pleasantly and not menacingly so. I also remember the Prime Minister, Chief Leabua Jonathan, driving up and down the main street in a huge black Mercedes with motorcycle outriders. He must have done so more to impress the population with his power than to arrive anywhere, because he went back and forth without apparent destination. He had once been elected to power democratically but refused to be dis-elected, if I may so put it, by the same means. For him, election's arrow flew in only one direction.

The medicine murders of which the author of the report

writes were not new but of late had become more frequent. They were the consequence of the belief that human body parts could be rendered into powerful medicine, either to bring good luck or prevent bad, including that wrought by the malevolence of rivals or enemies. It was not cannibalism in the strictest sense: human flesh was not consumed as such but was made into ointments and the like. At least, that is what the author says, and he gives the impression of being a careful man.

But why the increase in prevalence of such murders? It seems that the murders were carried out by, or on the orders of, the lesser chiefs, that is to say the lower rungs of the Basuto upper or ruling class, the victims being persons of lower social class but known for some desirable characteristic or quality. Why did the class of lesser chiefs resort to murder, though?

Lesser chiefs were appointed by higher chiefs and held office by their grace and favour. They had access to land for their private use and also had the right to demand labour from the population under their jurisdiction, though traditionally they used their privileges for the good of that population. With increased individualism, however, and the increase in the population, their privileged position became precarious. It was normal for higher level chiefs to 'place' their sons as lower-level chiefs, and with an increase in polygamy and the number of such sons to be 'placed', the number of places had also to be increased, to the detriment of the incumbent lesser chiefs, who lost status and income. The newly-'placed' were superior in the hierarchy, thanks to the protection of the higher chiefs, and therefore the lower chiefs resorted to the most powerful 'medicine' known in order to preserve them from ill-fortune or to harm the interlopers (often the same thing). Sometimes the lower chiefs participated in the murders themselves; more often, they were carried out by posses acting at their behest.

The colonial authorities saw the problem of the increase in the number of placemen to 'place', but of course their attempt to reduce it promptly doubled it. This is in accord with the only law that I have ever formulated for myself (though others may well have formulated it before me), namely that all attempts to decrease bureaucracy increase it. And even at its very early development as a modern polity, with a small, centralised budget, one can see the cloud of bureaucracy on the horizon. The budget of the Basutoland government in 1945 was divided in two heads, administrative and developmental. The expenditure of the first was £106,087 and of the second £17,613 — and even the latter, as Mr Jones pointed out, included a high proportion of administrative cost. A passage in the report reminded me of our hypertrophied public administration. The chiefs, both greater and smaller, exploited their courts by giving people vexatious and unnecessary administrative orders, and when they failed to carry them out fining them heavily for disobedience. The Basuto were pioneers of modern government.

A typical medicine murder consisted of an abduction to a remote place by a gang, a beating to death and the removal of body parts, not necessarily in that order. The body would then be thrown over a cliff or precipice to make the death look accidental. Investigation was very difficult because of the omertà of people towards their chiefs and the inability of the authorities to protect witnesses from the wrath of the guilty, who more often than not would be acquitted for lack of evidence. How primitive, one is tempted to exclaim: but I remember reading a few years ago that 30 per cent of criminal prosecutions in Britain collapse because of the intimidation of witnesses. Many of my patients, the victims of horrible crimes, would tell me that the perpetrator had told them that they should remember that he would be walking the same streets as they in a few weeks' time, even if convicted. Derisory sentences for serious crimes emboldened criminals. London is Lesotho.

Despite his analysis of the sociological causes of the increase in the Medicine murders, Mr Jones, in his conclusion, is quite clear about the role of ideas and beliefs in the situation. The quasi-economic analysis that he gives is not that of the final cause, *à la Marx*:

> The primary cause... of these murders is the general belief of the Basuto... in the efficacy of magical concoctions, usually termed "medicines," and their particular belief... in these protective medicines which are compounded from human flesh... Until it is realised that such medicines are incapable of performing the function attributed to them there will always be a certain number of people who will value them more highly than they do human life...

Three days before I write this, I read in the French newspaper, *Libération*, of a case of cannibalism in the Congo. In the midst of an ethnic conflict, pitting the Tutsi against the others, or rather the other way round, a Tutsi man was murdered, incinerated and partly eaten, obviously as a manifestation of

251

magical thinking. And the idea that human flesh confers special powers on those who consume it, either orally or in ointment, is obviously but the mirror image of our own feeling that human bodies are not to be treated as just another inanimate object. A very old American doctor with not long to live, a strict rationalist with an abomination of religion in all its forms, once wrote to me to say that he hoped after his death to be thrown away just like any other piece of rubbish. As an ambition, this appalled me, and I am not easily appalled.

It is, of course, but a short step from witch-doctoring and superstition to psychoanalysis, the religious movement started by one of the great cult-leaders of the past century, Sigmund Freud. Abandon hope all ye who enter one of his prolonged case reports — for example, that of the Wolf Man, Sergius Konstantinovich Pankeyev, often regarded as the most important of them.

One enters immediately a labyrinth of hypotheses claimed as established facts, *ad hominem* argumentation against those who dare to disagree with the author, self-contradiction, special pleading, implausibility, absurdity and outright lies (as well as omissions so egregious that they count as outright lies), all recounted with an air of authority earned by prolonged previous study.

Any medical student who presented a case as Freud presents that of the Wolf Man would be (rightly) halted within seconds of starting, for Freud's mode of presentation is so disordered that after more than a hundred pages one is still not quite sure what Freud was trying to treat or what the actual complaints of the patient were. Of course, this method of exposition has the great advantage that it makes any assessment of the success or otherwise of the treatment difficult and the refutation of Freud's claims all but impossible. But even if it were possible from Freud's account to determine the success or failure of the treatment, the psychoanalysts would move the goalposts in the event of failure. The aim of treatment, they would say, is not *cure* (a rather vulgar concept) but *understanding*, especially at a theoretical level. Who cares whether the patient is better or worse or the same? Such considerations are for the naïve and unsophisticated. In fact, vulgar attempts at corroborating Freud's therapeutic claims with regard to many of his cases establish that he was not merely mistaken but a liar.

The Wolf Man was a rich Russian aristocrat whom Freud successfully fleeced by seeing him six days a week for more than four years, at a huge fee each time, though no doubt at the cost to himself of boredom. The Wolf Man is so-called because he had, according to Freud, a wolf phobia, but the only evidence for this that Freud mentions is that he once had a nightmare, at the age of about four, of wolves sitting in the walnut tree outside his bedroom and that he used, for a time, to be very afraid of the picture of a wolf in a children's book that his older children used to show him. Omitted from Freud's account — and this omission can hardly have been accidental — is the fact that the estate on which the Wolf Man was brought up had many wolves which no doubt could be heard at night and of which his father was an enthusiastic hunter, surrounding himself triumphantly with their corpses.

(Incidentally, the great majority of human victims of wolves, at least in France between the seventeenth and twentieth centuries, were women and children, so that it would not have been altogether irrational for children to be afraid of wolves, and indeed it might have been irrational *not* to be afraid of them.) But apart from these two instances, there is nothing to suggest a wolf-phobia at all; nor in Freud's clinical description, insofar as it can be described as a description, is there any awareness that anything more is necessary. His way of writing represented an astonishing regression by comparison with French and German psychiatrists of the nineteenth century.

At many turns one finds evidence of Freud's intellectual dishonesty. He is like a swindler who carries out his swindles in the plain sight of those whom he swindles (and other witnesses). For example, the following admission would immediately suggest that Freud was engaged in a kind of brain-washing rather than a disinterested enquiry. 'It required a long education,' he wrote, 'to induce him [the Wolf Man] to take an independent share of this work...'Or again, 'So analyses such as this [of the Wolf Man] are not published in order to produce conviction in the minds of those whose attitude has hitherto been recusant and sceptical...' Of the gathering of corroborative evidence for his surmises, for example of the patient's early memories, many of which were insinuated into his mind by Freud where he did not make them up out of whole cloth, he says, 'It may be tempting to take the easy course of filling up the gaps in a patient's memory by making enquiries from the older members of his family; but I cannot advise too strongly against such a technique.' In any case, Freud said repeatedly that the difference between what really happened and what the patient said happened was of no significance to him; he is one of the founding fathers, or patron saints, of what might be called the *My truth* school of thought. When he says at the outset of his account of the Wolf Man, 'I am unable to give a purely historical or purely theoretical account of my patient's story; I can write a history neither of the treatment nor the illness, but I shall find myself obliged to combine the two methods of presentation,' he does not condescend to explain *why* he cannot or *what* obliges him. In fact, by the end of his combined method, the reader feels that his mind has been put through a psychoanalytical food mixer and that it is difficult to grasp anything clearly about the case. How does one go about discussing, let along arguing with, the following?

> It is easy to make a unified statement of what was expressed on the one hand by the complaint he made and on the other hand by the single exceptional condition under that which the complaint no longer held good, and thus to make clear the whole meaning that underlay the two factors; he wished he could be back in the womb, not simply that he might be reborn, but in order that he might be completed within there by his father, might obtain sexual satisfaction from him, and might bear him a child.

You might as well say that that is why millions take the subway in New York, the Métro in Paris, and the underground in London, every day. But let Freud have the last word, as a true man of science (as he claimed to be):

The whale and the polar bear, it has been said, cannot wage war on each other, for since each is confined to his own element they cannot meet. It is just as impossible to argue with workers in the field of psychology or of the neuroses, who do not recognize the postulate of psychoanalysis and who look on its results as artefacts.

Having only one and a half pages left of my notebook to fill, it seems but right to devote them to Dylan Thomas, who gave me, nearly seventy years after his death, my title.

One of his greatest poems, *Poem on His Birthday*, was started, though not completed, in the month of my birth. Thomas was one of those people who play a role for too long, in his case that of the *poète maudit*, and become what they play: but in his case, he did not merely play at being a genius, he really *was* a genius. If A.E. Housman (a complex man who fought and suffered his way to simplicity, of expression if not of life) was right, and true poetry is what causes a shiver when you recite it to yourself, then Thomas was, very unusually among twentieth century poets, a true poet. The curious thing is that, even when his meaning is uncertain, he produces a profound emotional reaction. In my case, the effect is heightened by my visits to Laugharne, the small town in Carmarthenshire where Thomas lived in a house and had a writing shed overlooking the beautiful and peaceful estuary of the River Tawe. Another of his great birthday poems, *Poem in October*, captures the place and the scene to verbally inventive perfection. He begins:

It was my thirtieth year to heaven
Woke to my hearing from harbour and neighbour wood
And the mussel pooled and the heron
Priested shore
The morning beckon
With water praying and call of seagull and rock
And the knock of sailing boats on the net webbed wall…

The first line, *It was my thirtieth year to heaven*, stirs something deep in me, though the locution is odd. What precisely does it mean? That Thomas, now thirty years old, was nearer to death (but he did not believe, not overtly at any rate, in heaven or the afterlife)? That the kingdom of heaven was now within him? Unlikely, given the wilful turbulence of his life. That it was the thirtieth year of his search for perfection? Insofar as such a state of perfection can be imagined, though it cannot satisfy for long and is therefore by definition not *really* perfection, it is the Tawe estuary with its mussel pooled and heron priested shore. A single line of Thomas's can evoke a multitude of thoughts and feelings and does so with a verbal felicity that is in his case innate, God-given. True he laboured long to produce his poems, but however long I laboured, I could never come within a million miles of his poetry. I open his *Collected Poems* at random, and fall on *Especially when the October Wind*:

Especially when the October wind
With frosty fingers punishes my hair…
Especially when the October wind
With fists of turnips punishes the land…

257

Not all my words are equal to one line of this.

Printed in Great Britain
by Amazon